CATALYTIC GOVERNANCE

LEADING CHANGE IN THE INFORMATION AGE

Although the information age offers individuals the power to make their voices heard, we often end up with a cacophony of competing voices rather than a conversation. With so many people empowered to join the decision-making process, the diversity of stakeholders in governance situations poses a special challenge: How do you steer when so many hands are on the wheel?

Catalytic Governance offers a proven approach to managing this challenge, built on the insight that effective leadership and governance depends less on traditional top-down approaches and more on creating shared meanings and frameworks. Drawing on their experiences managing transformational change in complex, multi-stakeholder environments on issues ranging from finance to climate change, health, and the digital revolution, Patricia Meredith, Steven A. Rosell, and Ged R. Davis demonstrate how to use dialogue to engage stakeholders, explore alternative perspectives, develop shared mental maps and a vision of the future, and co-create strategies and initiatives to realize that future. While elements of this approach will be familiar, this is the first time they have been combined into a coherent model and tested together in practice. The book focuses on the case study of transforming the Canadian payments system

PATRICIA MEREDITH is a senior advisor on strategy and governance to corporate boards and management.

STEVEN A. ROSELL is the author of four books on dialogue-based leadership and governance.

GED R. DAVIS is an experienced scenario practitioner and strategist.

CATALYTIC GOVERNANCE

Leading Change in the Information Age

Patricia Meredith
Steven A. Rosell
Ged R. Davis

UNIVERSITY OF TORONTO PRESS
Toronto Buffalo London

Rotman-UTP Publishing
Toronto Buffalo London
www.utppublishing.com
Printed in the U.S.A.

ISBN 978-1-4426-4941-5 (cloth)
ISBN 978-1-4426-2676-8 (paper)

Printed on acid-free, 100% post-consumer recycled paper with vegetable-based inks.

Library and Archives Canada Cataloguing in Publication

Meredith, Patricia, 1955–, author
Catalytic governance : leading change in the information age /
Patricia Meredith, Steven A. Rosell, Ged R. Davis.

Includes bibliographical references and index.
ISBN 978-1-4426-4941-5 (cloth). – ISBN 978-1-4426-2676-8 (paper)

1. Transformational leadership.   2. Information society.   3. Corporate
governance.   4. Public administration.   I. Rosell, Steven A., author
II. Davis, Ged R., 1943–, author   III. Title.

HD57.7.M47 2016   658.4'092   C2015-908384-2

University of Toronto Press acknowledges the financial assistance to its
publishing program of the Canada Council for the Arts and the Ontario Arts
Council, an agency of the Government of Ontario.

ONTARIO ARTS COUNCIL
CONSEIL DES ARTS DE L'ONTARIO
an Ontario government agency
un organisme du gouvernement de l'Ontario

Canada Council Conseil des Arts
for the Arts   du Canada

Funded by the   Financé par le
Government   gouvernement
of Canada   du Canada

Contents

Acknowledgments

This journey would not have been possible without the support and contributions of many people, only some of whom we can mention here. In particular, we would like to thank the late James Flaherty, Minister of Finance in the previous federal government, whose vision and support created the opportunity for us to undertake this journey. He was the ultimate catalyst in transforming the Canadian payments system.

He agreed to establish a Payments Task Force whose members were diverse, had much relevant experience and expertise, but were not the usual industry insiders. He sanctioned the Payments Roundtable process that the task force wanted to use to bring together a wide range of stakeholders (including senior executives from banks and other financial institutions, technology and telecommunications companies, and especially retailers, consumers, and other users) to work together to understand one another's perspectives and the disruptive changes underway in payments worldwide. He supported efforts to make the work of the task force available online to anyone who wanted to engage, and allowed the task force to present a "Proposed Governance Framework" for comment and collaboration months before it was officially recommended to him. In his final budget presented to Parliament in March 2014, he tabled legislation to overhaul the payments system and the governance of the Canadian Payments Association.

We would also like to thank the members of the Payments Task Force – Brad Badeau, Stephane Le Bouyonnec, John Chant, Laura

Gillham, Lili de Grandpré, and Terry Wright – who thought they were agreeing to attend a few meetings, review some research, evaluate some options, and make a few recommendations. Instead they dedicated countless hours of their time, immersing themselves in the payments community, visualizing alternative futures for the Canadian payments system, and chairing working and advisory groups to develop and implement the most desirable scenario.

The members of the Payments Roundtable played a critical role in transforming the Canadian payments system. As described in this volume, they explored different perspectives, challenged our underlying assumptions and beliefs about the future of payments, established a shared language, created alternative plausible futures based upon a range of differing assumptions, and formed a "coalition of the willing" to try to enact the most desirable scenario. Together with the members of the Payments Task Force, they are in a real sense co-authors of this effort (although they are not responsible for the writing of this book or for any errors or omissions it may contain).

Dr Daniel Coates provided wise counsel throughout this effort, drawing on decades of experience as both a senior government official and a political adviser. He played a leading role in organizing and supporting the Payments Roundtable that is at the centre of the case study described in this volume. No less importantly, he was one of the first to review the manuscript of this book, providing constructive criticism and insightful comments that did much to strengthen the final result.

Aran Hamilton helped us navigate the intricacies of mobile payments, emerging currencies, and digital identification and authentication. He enabled our understanding of the implications of cloud computing, smart devices, and mobile Internet for payments – no easy task. Aran supported the mobile payments and digital identification and authentication working groups and has continued as Interim President of the Digital Identification and Authentication Council of Canada (DIACC). Finally, we would like to thank Aran for reviewing the technology sections of this book.

The Secretariat of the Task Force (Kevin Wright, Kym Shumsky, Brendan Carley, Sophie Lefebvre, and Margitt Herrmann) also played an invaluable role. They came to the Payments Task Force with expectations based on previous task forces and worked very hard to adapt to a new and dramatically different process. Viewpoint Learning (especially Daniel Coates, Heidi Gantwerk, Isabella Furth, and Patricia Davis) supported and facilitated the dialogue and scenarios process for the Payments Roundtable. Without that, change would not have been possible, because "Progress is impossible without change and those who cannot change their minds cannot change anything."[*]

The consultants who assisted the working and advisory groups to develop the initiatives to co-create the desired scenario included Phil Bruno, Danish Yusuf, and Eric Montiero from McKinsey and Company; and Jacques St Amand, Judy McCreery, and Denise Ellis. They did the research and documented the initiatives that were passed on to the Ministry of Finance and the Canadian Payments Association.

Finally and most importantly, we would like to thank those who have helped us to write this book. Isabella Furth did an amazing job of making our three very different voices sound like one. Three anonymous reviewers gave us invaluable feedback and helped to improve the manuscript immeasurably. And last but not least, our editor Jennifer DiDomenico at University of Toronto Press provided welcome guidance, encouragement, and constructive criticism as we finalized this book.

---

[*] The aphorism is attributed to George Bernard Shaw.

Glossary of Key Terms and Acronyms

ABM.   Automatic banking machine.

ACH.   Automated Clearing House. An electronic network for payments in the United States. ACH processes large volumes of credit and debit transactions, including payments from the federal government, public and private payrolls, and bill payments.

ACSS.   Automated Clearing Settlement System. ACSS is the system through which the vast majority of payment items in Canada are cleared, including paper-based payment items such as cheques and electronic items such as pre-authorized debits and direct deposits. ACSS handles 99 per cent of the Canadian Payments Association (CPA) daily payment volume: nearly 24 million payments on an average business day. But, since most of these payments are for relatively small amounts, this volume accounts for only about 12 per cent of the total value cleared using the CPA systems. Most of the total value is cleared via the Large Value Transfer System (LVTS; see below).

APCA.   Australian Payments Clearing Association.

B2B.   Business-to-business. B2B payments are payments between businesses: for example,

	payments between a manufacturer and a supplier of parts or raw materials, or between a wholesaler and a retailer. In Canada, most B2B payments are carried out by means of paper cheques.
B2C.	Business-to-consumer. B2C payments are payments between businesses and end consumers, such as retail purchases or service purchases. B2C payments can be made in many ways including cash, cheque, credit, debit, or online.
B2G.	Business to government.
C2B.	Consumer-to-business.
CEO.	Chief executive officer.
chip and PIN.	A technology for credit and debit cards in which card information is stored on embedded microchips rather than on the magnetic stripes currently common in Canada and the United States. The chip is protected by high-level encryption and is almost impossible to copy, making these cards more secure than magnetic stripe cards. When using these cards, cardholders authenticate their information using a personal identification number (PIN).
CIO.	Chief information officer.
cloud computing.	A pay-per-use model for enabling available, convenient, on-demand network access to a shared pool of configurable computing resources (for example, networks, servers, data storage, applications, services) that can be rapidly provisioned and released with minimal management effort or service provider interaction.
contactless cards.	Plastic cards that communicate with a terminal (for example, a payment terminal) via

	radio waves. When used for credit or debit payments, contactless cards need only come within a few inches of the payment terminal; they do not need to be physically swiped.
COTW.	Coalition of the willing.
CPA.	Canadian Payments Association.
CPC.	Canadian Payments Council.
CPS.	Canadian payments system.
DIA.	Digital identification and authentication
DIY.	Do-it-yourself.
EDI.	Electronic data interchange.
e-wallet.	A digital "wallet" application on a computer or smart phone. E-wallets securely store and transmit information needed for online or mobile payments, including passwords; PINs; credit, debit, and prepaid card information; and electronic cash.
EFT.	Electronic funds transfer.
EIPP.	Electronic invoice presentment and payment. Electronic billing, usually in the context of B2B or B2C payments.
EMV.	Europay, MasterCard, and Visa. A global standard for chip-based credit and debit cards that allows cards made by different companies to be securely used and authenticated at a wide range of point-of-sale terminals and ABMs.
FCAC.	Financial Consumer Agency of Canada.
FDC.	First Data Corporation.
FI.	Financial institution.
GDP.	Gross domestic product.
ID.	Identification, identity, or identifier.
Interac.	Canada's electronic debit card network.

Interchange fee.   A fee that forms the bulk of the "acceptance fee" paid by a merchant when accepting payment using a credit card network (e.g., MasterCard, Visa, AMEX). Most of the interchange fee flows to the card issuer.

ISO.   International Organization for Standardization

IT.   Information technology.

LVTS.   Large Value Transfer System. LVTS is an electronic funds transfer system that allows Canadian financial institutions to send large payments back and forth to each other securely and in real time, including Government of Canada payments. LVTS is operated by the CPA, and settlement is guaranteed. While the Automated Clearing Settlement System (ACSS) handles the most volume of payments moving through the system, LVTS handles the most value. In 2010, LVTS processed an average of about 24,000 payments a day, worth an average total of $149 billion – about 88 per cent of the total value of payments cleared through the CPA each day.

Mobile payment.   Any payment (cash, debit, credit) made using a smart phone or portable computing device, including over the Internet or using near-field communication (NFC; see below) technology.

NACHA.   The U.S. National Automated Clearing House Association, formed in 1974 as a not-for-profit association to collaborate on standards for the Automated Clearing House (ACH), administers and facilitates private-sector operating rules for ACH payments, which define the roles and responsibilities of financial institutions and other ACH network participants.

NFC.   Near-field communication. A contactless technology that allows devices such as mobile

	phones to communicate wirelessly with other devices, such as payment terminals, and other phones over short distances (5 to 10 cm). NFC chips are increasingly common features in smart phones.
OSFI.	Office of the Superintendent of Financial Institutions. OSFI is the primary regulator and supervisor of federally regulated deposit-taking institutions, insurance companies, and federally regulated private pension plans.
P2P.	Person-to-person. P2P payments are a counterpart to B2B (business-to-business) payments, but are made between individuals. In Canada, most P2P payments are made by cheque or cash.
PARC.	Palo Alto Research Center.
PIN.	Personal identification number.
POS.	Point of sale.
PWGSC.	Public Works and Government Services Canada
RTGS.	Real time gross settlement.
SEPA.	Single European Payments Area.
SGO.	Self-governing organization.
SMEs.	Small and medium-sized enterprises.
STP.	Straight-through processing. A process through which transactions are processed automatically to eliminate the time and cost of manually keying in the information. STP is completed in hours, minutes, or even seconds – far faster than the three to five days currently required for traditional paper-based processing.
SWIFT.	Society for Worldwide Interbank Financial Telecommunication.

Transformative change.

Change that is profound, fundamental, and irreversible. It is a radical shift in thinking, assumptions, perception, and viewpoint – change that precludes a return to previous mental maps and that leads to large alterations in external behaviour.

TSYS.

Total System Services, Inc.

Members of the Payments Roundtable

(Asterisks indicate members of the Payments Task Force)

* Brad Badeau: Senior Vice-president and CFO, Burgundy Asset Management
James Baumgartner: President and CEO, Moneris
Sonia Baxendale: Senior Executive Vice-president and President, CIBC Retail Markets, CIBC
Diane Brisebois: President and CEO, Retail Council of Canada
* John Chant: Professor Emeritus, Simon Fraser University
Patrice Dagenais: Vice-president, Payments and Business Partnerships, Desjardins Group
* Lili de Grandpré: Managing Director, CenCEO Conseil
Betty DeVita: President, MasterCard Canada
Steve Doucette: Vice-president, Controller, Sun Life
Trudy Fahie/Jamie McEwen: President and CEO/Chief Marketing Officer, Walmart Bank Canada *(counted as one member)*
Philip Fayer: President and CEO, Pivotal Payments
Brian Fox: Senior Vice-president and General Manager, Business Management, Western Union Canada
* Laura Gilham: Vice-president, Marketing and Customer Strategy, Empire Theatres Limited
Brien Gray: Executive Vice-president, Canadian Federation of Independent Business
Aran Hamilton: Adviser to the Task Force for the Payments System Review

Kevin Higa: Chief Financial Officer, Running Room
Tim Hockey/Paul Vessey: President and CEO/Executive
Vice-president, TD Canada Trust (*counted as one member*)
Mike Kitchen: Senior Vice-president of Card and Retail Payment
Services, BMO Bank of Montreal
Drazen Lalovic: Vice-president of Business Planning and
Development, Telus
* **Stephane Le Bouyonnec:** President, Synergis Capital
Almis Ledas: Vice-president, Corporate Development, Bell
Mobility
Guy Legault: President and CEO, Canadian Payments Association
Réjean Lévesque: Executive Vice-president, Personal and
Commercial Banking, Banque Nationale
Andrew MacIsaac: Vice-president, Retail Controls and Indirect
Procurement, Loblaw
Darrell MacMullin: General Manager, PayPal Canada
* **Patricia Meredith:** Professional Associate and Senior Adviser,
Monitor Group Canada
Mark O'Connell: President and CEO, Interac
Gillian Riley: Senior Vice-president and Head of Retail
Payments, Deposits, and Lending, ScotiaBank
Dave Robinson: Vice-president, Emerging Products, Rogers
Don Rolfe/Oscar van der Meer: President and CEO/ Chief
Technology and Payments Officer, Central One (*counted as one
member*)
Jacques St. Amant: Canadian Consumer Initiative
Barbara Stymiest: Group Head, Strategy, Treasury and Corporate
Services, RBC
Vince Timpano: President and CEO, Aeroplan
Jim Tobin: Senior Vice-president and General Manager, Software
and Services, Research in Motion (Blackberry)
Ernie Wallace: Executive Director, Prestocard
Tim Wilson: Head of Visa Canada, Visa
Greg Wolfond: Chair and CEO, Securekey
* **W. Terry Wright, QC:** Counsel, Pitblado LLP
Mark Zelmer: Chief, Financial Stability Department, Bank
of Canada

CATALYTIC GOVERNANCE

Leadership and Governance in the Information Age

It has been quite a journey. This is the story of a major effort to devise and implement transformative changes to Canada's payments system (CPS). It began in a relatively traditional way but became a case study of developing better approaches to leading and governing in the information age.

The information age[1] is accelerating the pace of change and threatening to overwhelm methods of governance that were designed for a world of slower change, more limited information flow, and clearer boundaries. To succeed in this more complex, interconnected, and rapidly changing world, people in all sectors are recognizing the urgent need for approaches to leadership and governance that are inclusive,[2] dialogue-based, forward looking, and action-oriented. These are approaches that can enable systems to adapt more quickly than previously and operate more effectively across the shifting boundaries between organizations, industries, disciplines, sectors, and political jurisdictions. A society or organization's ability to prosper in this world of rapid change will depend, in no small measure, on its ability to develop these new leadership and governance capacities.[3]

One such approach is detailed in this book. *Catalytic Governance* describes a process for leading transformative change that engages a wide range of stakeholders in dialogue and empowers them to envisage and enact a desired future.[4]

Catalytic Governance

The word "governance" derives from the Greek *kybernan* (to steer) and *kybernetes* (pilot or helmsman). Governance is the process whereby an organization or society steers itself. While government is central to the process of governance in society, in the information age government is increasingly only one helmsman among many, as more and more players – voluntary organizations, interest groups, the private sector, the media, and more – become involved in that process. To steer effectively when so many hands (with so many different agendas) are on the wheel, a more catalytic approach to governance is needed.

Our understanding of "leadership" has undergone a similar shift in recent years, as the literature shifts away from a focus on the traits and practices of the effective leader and towards a focus on leadership as a process or function within a group. Leadership in the information age is a process of making meaning – the process of making sense of what people are doing together so that people will understand and feel committed. This is a process that is dialogue based and in which many individuals can participate.[5]

The model described in *Catalytic Governance* emphasizes that a wider range of stakeholders needs to be involved in the governance process in the information age, and that governments, boards, and other governing bodies need to make room for those players. This means that governments and boards must relax day-to-day control (or the illusion of such control) and shift to a catalytic role.

In a seminal article, Harlan Cleveland eloquently describes why a catalytic approach to leadership and governance is essential in the information age:

> In an information-rich polity [or organization], the very definition of control changes. Very large numbers of people empowered by knowledge assert the right or feel the obligation to "make policy." Decision-making proceeds not by "recommendations up, orders down," but by development of a shared sense of direction among those who must form the parade if there is going to be a parade ... Real-life "planning" is the dynamic improvisation by the many on a general sense of

direction – announced by the few, but only after genuine consultation with those who will have to improvise on it. Participation and public feedback become conditions precedent to decisions that stick.[6]

In this process the core roles of governments and boards remain as important as ever – in particular the responsibility to define and protect the broader public interest, including that of the voiceless (in the case of governments), or to ensure that actions are taken in the best interests of the corporation (in the case of boards). In both cases there is a longer-term stewardship responsibility, including a responsibility to future generations. That public interest or corporate interest cannot be reduced to the sum of stakeholder interests. What changes is not these fundamental responsibilities of governments or boards but how they can accomplish them effectively in the information age, in particular when transformative change is required.

Another reason we need catalytic governance processes is that the information age increasingly presents us with "wicked problems." A wicked problem has innumerable causes, is tough to describe, and does not have one right answer. It cannot be addressed with a purely scientific/rational approach because it lacks a clear definition of what the problem is; and it is difficult to tackle because effective and legitimate action requires the support of multiple stakeholders with widely differing perspectives and priorities.[7] Examples of wicked problems include climate change, health care, terrorism, inequality, and many business strategy issues.[8]

The catalytic governance model represents an important step forward in developing a practical approach to addressing such intractable challenges, and is designed for the interconnected and rapidly changing world of the information age.

Through the work described in this volume, we have further developed and tested the catalytic governance process to produce a model that has five steps. These are summarized in figure 0.1 and described in more detail in chapter 6.

Step 1: Frame the Problem and Set Boundaries for Solutions: Governments, boards, or other governing bodies (as stewards) take the initial step of framing the problem and agenda, defining

Figure 0.1: The Catalytic Governance Model

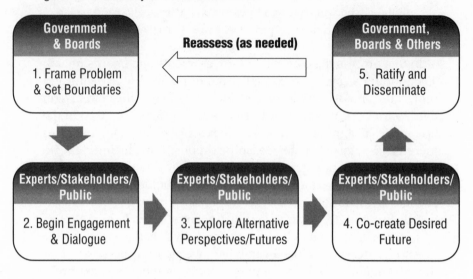

the process to be followed and the range of stakeholders to be included, and setting the boundaries for acceptable solutions.
Step 2: Begin Engagement and Dialogue: Governing bodies engage a wide range of stakeholders around the issue, embedding the ground rules of dialogue and engagement in all conversations from the outset. Governing bodies need to ensure that all the key stakeholders and viewpoints are included in the process, including those normally underrepresented. The stakeholders should be selected to be a microcosm of the system at issue, not just representatives of particular interests. In a true dialogue, participants need to be free to speak for themselves, not as representatives. A continuing and expanding process of dialogue and engagement is fundamental to catalytic governance.

Step 3: Explore Alternative Perspectives/Futures: Participants in the process explore in detail a variety of perspectives on the issue and alternative possibilities for how it may unfold in the future. This provides a way for participants to understand and learn from others' points of view, and to start to see the limitations of their own. Ensuring that multiple viewpoints are taken into account creates a richer view of the issue and its possibilities.

Step 4: Co-create the Desired Future: Those stakeholders who are willing define their more desired future and develop practical action steps to realize that future. Often this will require a process of action learning – taking experimental actions and learning from the result. To be effective, the stakeholder group must include key individuals in a position to bring about change and willing to take action.

Step 5: Ratify and Disseminate the Desired Future: Governments, boards, and other governing bodies play a leading role, first by ratifying and disseminating the result of the catalytic governance process, and then by acting and encouraging action on the emerging strategy (including legislating if necessary) and monitoring the results. This step is not a simple, once-and-for-all end point; it is itself the start of a new process of action learning.

Task Force for the Payments System Review

In this book we use the transformation of Canada's payment system as a rich case study of catalytic governance. The reform effort was sparked by years of stakeholder complaints about the lack of information provided by the Canadian payments system and its high cost. Small and medium-sized businesses were upset about the escalating merchant discount fees on credit cards; individuals were perplexed by the myriad rules, regulations, and service charges for small payments; large corporations complained that existing systems could not carry enough information for them to automate the processing of their receivables and payables. New entrants were concerned about access to payments systems infrastructure and the uncertainty created by a patchwork of regulations. And

Canada did not have a plan to move from paper-based payments (cash and cheques) to digital immediate funds transfer.

On 18 June 2010, James Flaherty, Canada's Minister of Finance, announced the members of the Task Force for the Payments System Review (Payments Task Force). The chair was a non-partisan former senior bank executive and strategy adviser to financial services and technology companies. The members of the task force were selected for their expert backgrounds and demographic diversity[9] and deliberately did not include any traditional payments players, such as banks and networks. Already this represented a significant departure from previous such efforts.

Minister Flaherty mandated the Payments Task Force to "conduct a review, given the importance of a safe and efficient payments system, to ensure that the framework supporting the Canadian payments system remains effective in light of new participants and innovation." Payments are everywhere. From coffee purchased at a coin-operated machine to the daily exchange of billions of dollars among corporations, financial institutions, and governments, the transfer of value underpins our economy. Every year, Canadians make more than 25 billion payments, worth more than 45 trillion dollars. These payments allow people to run households, make it possible for businesses and other organizations to operate, and let governments fund essential programs. But the payments business is undergoing a dramatic shift. Just as the Industrial Revolution brought massive change in production and manufacturing, the information revolution is changing our payments system.

Given the complexity, rapid change, and resulting uncertainties of the payments environment, the task force recognized that a traditional approach (conducting research, hearing stakeholder and expert opinions, and then making recommendations) would not be adequate. Instead it chose to make dialogue its guiding principle and called on consumers, industry, government, and businesses to work together to build the payments system we need. To focus that dialogue and to explore alternative plausible futures for the Canadian payments system (CPS), the task force helped to convene and participated in a Payments Roundtable. When a "coalition of the willing" emerged from the roundtable, ready and able to develop initiatives to co-create the most desired future, the task force provided resources to support stakeholder working and advisory groups to begin to realize that future.

As described in the following pages, what transpired over eighteen months was transformative, as mindsets shifted and mental maps were redrawn. What began as forty leaders with different and sometimes conflicting agendas and perspectives became the core of an energized and more inclusive "payments industry," with group members working together to make the governance and other changes needed to take the CPS into the digital age.

Having experienced this dramatic progress on the complex and intractable issues of the CPS in so short a time, we began to ask ourselves whether the process we had followed could produce similar results on other "wicked problems." That possibility led us to write this book.

Catalytic Governance is written for leaders in the public and private sectors who are looking for more effective ways to initiate transformative change and to tackle wicked problems in the information age, and for students of leadership and governance in universities and the media.

The Shape of This Book

Catalytic Governance presents a detailed model of a more catalytic approach to governance – one that is designed for the realities of the information age and the need to tackle wicked problems. It also describes how this model was developed and tested in a major effort to lead change in the Canadian payments system.

Chapter 1 sets the stage by summarizing the interplay of social and technological changes that define the information age, the particular challenges facing the Canadian payments system, and the need for new forms of governance and leadership.

Chapter 2 introduces the Task Force for the Payments System Review (Payments Task Force) and the mandate it was given by the Minister of Finance – the *first step* in the catalytic governance model. It then describes the effort of the Payments Task Force to engage a wide range of stakeholders in an open, inclusive, and transparent dialogue – the *second step* of the catalytic governance model. The chapter also describes the special form of dialogue central to this effort, to the model, and to the "magic": a method that enabled stakeholders to get on the same page, find a surprising amount of common ground, and begin to think of themselves as the "Canadian payments industry" – a concept that had not existed prior to the work of the Payments Task Force.

Chapter 3 describes the Payments Roundtable, which was created to explore different perspectives and challenge underlying assumptions and beliefs about the future of payments, to establish a shared language, and to create alternative plausible futures for the Canadian payments system based upon different assumptions. (This is the *third step* of the catalytic governance model.) Through the roundtable process, participants from a wide range of sectors and with different connections to the payments system deepened their understanding of the issues they all faced in adapting to advancing digital technologies. Armed with this shared understanding, they were able to frame a number of scenarios to explore the challenges faced by a nascent "payments industry" – scenarios that formed the basis for a new understanding of the issues and new ways forward. In the process, what had started as an inchoate group – whose members had a wide range of interests, perspectives, and agendas – became a cohesive community focused on realizing transformative change.

As the Payments Roundtable was unfolding, the task force began a parallel effort to develop a new governance framework for payments. As described in chapter 4, this process began with a more traditional strategy/policy-development approach, which was not successful: none of the resulting governance options seemed likely to be effective in dealing with the dramatic challenges facing the system (and indeed some had been tried before without success). At the same time, the inclusive, dialogue-based, forward-looking, and action-oriented process of the task force and roundtable was proving to be far more effective. So the catalytic governance process of the task force and roundtable became the model for a "Proposed Governance Framework" that was developed and refined by working and advisory groups before being recommended to Minister Flaherty in December 2011.

The insight, energy, and sense of ownership created through the roundtable process also inspired a large group of its members to commit themselves to realizing one of the scenarios: a vision of the future in which Canada becomes a world leader in payments. Almost immediately, this self-described "coalition of the willing" began the practical work of drafting and testing initiatives to transition Canada from paper-based to digital payments, including building a digital identification and authentication regime, implementing electronic invoicing and payments for business and government, creating a public-private mobile ecosystem, and upgrading Canada's clearing and settlement infrastructure. The development and testing of these strategies – the *fourth step* in the catalytic governance model – and the dissemination and response by the federal government – the *fifth step* in the model – are outlined in chapter 5.

In our concluding chapter, we use the lessons learned from the Payments Task Force experience to provide a more detailed description of catalytic governance. We also describe areas where more work is needed to further develop the model, as well as examples of subject areas where it could be applied.

The catalytic governance process uses dialogue to engage stakeholders, explore alternative perspectives or scenarios, develop shared mental maps and a vision of the future, and co-create strategies and initiatives to realize that future. It creates governance that is inclusive, learning-based, and action-oriented. It is designed to address the wicked problems and governance challenges we face in the interconnected and rapidly changing society of the information age.

We hope that the experience described in this book and the lessons we learned along the way will be helpful to others facing their own wicked problems and seeking to improve leadership and governance in the information age.

The Global Information Society

An "information society" is not simply a society that uses information technology. Rather, it is a social, economic, and political order
that arises from the interplay of social and technological dynamics.

We have seen many of these dynamics play out at first hand over
the past few decades. Enormous advances in information processing
and telecommunications have given rise to the mobile Internet, social networking, cloud computing, smart devices, and an explosion
in e-commerce. The structure of work is changing as the economy
becomes more globalized and more knowledge-based. The media –
both traditional media and social media – have a vastly expanded
role and reach. Much of the population has greater access to education, information, and the ability to organize,[1] giving rise to a range
of stakeholder groups hoping to assert a role in governance. And we
have a much richer infrastructure of public and private organizations – as well as greater collaboration and contention among them.

The "information society" that results from this ferment is richly
interconnected and complex: everything seems connected to everything else. The vast increase in information availability also brings
greater overload, filtering, and denial,[2] compresses both time and
space, and intensifies turbulence and unpredictability.

Many of these changes have powerful implications for the process of governance. For example:

- The globalizing economy has created interconnected stock exchanges, borderless capital markets, global supply chains, and
  a push for businesses to operate on a regional or international

scale. More and more issues – including trade, the environment, and human rights – must be handled by networks and organizations that transcend national boundaries.

- At the same time, we are seeing a trend towards atomization, democratization, and fragmentation. As regionalism grows and multinational states fragment, sub-national governments wield increasing power. Every nation and organization must take more and more voices into account as more groups organize to assert a role in the process of governance.[3]
- We are shifting away from a hierarchical, "command and control" model of organization. In both the public and private sectors, organizations are downsizing, stripping away middle management, and contracting out or privatizing work. Increasingly, they rely on networks, task forces, and other flexible, decentralized, "client-centred" ways of organizing.
- Leaner, less centralized organizations rely ever more heavily on human resources. Both public and private sector organizations increasingly depend on well-qualified staff who can manage large amounts of information, establish effective working relationships within and outside the organization, make independent judgments, and innovate.
- The increased flow of information makes secrecy ever more elusive: information runs through so many channels and access is so widespread that leaks have become almost standard. This has serious implications for governing systems that rely on a certain degree of confidentiality.[4]
- We are also witnessing a fundamental restructuring of longstanding categories. Historical boundaries are blurring and changing – between industries, between the public and private sectors, and even between states. As these entities search for new relationships and alliances, basic conceptual distinctions are being called into question.

While the term "information society" often conjures images of the technologies so central to its emergence, its true hallmark is the growing degree of interconnection that is emerging, both within the state and across national boundaries. An increasingly interconnected society dissolves familiar boundaries. But boundaries are fundamental to identity, to organization, to culture, and to governance. So the challenge of governance becomes a continual process of trying to redefine those boundaries and develop more effective ways to work across them.

As boundaries blur and change, and as basic conceptual distinctions need to be rethought, we are exploring a territory for which there is no reliable map. We usually describe our inability to make sense of proliferating and unfamiliar information in terms of information overload. But the problem may be instead that our existing frameworks and methods of interpretation – our existing mental maps – are inadequate to translate the wealth of data and information into meaningful knowledge.

Harlan Cleveland offers a useful way of conceptualizing the difficulty: *Data*, he says, are unrefined ore, undifferentiated facts without contexts. *Information* is refined ore – data that are organized but that we have not yet internalized. It is the newspapers we have not yet read, or the course of study we have not yet taken. *Knowledge*, however, is information we have internalized and integrated with our own frameworks.[5] This formulation suggests that in an information society, effective governance initiates the process of translating data and information into knowledge: interpreting the data, giving them meaning, and so making them useful as a basis for action.[6]

Information and Communications Technology

Although the ubiquity of information and communications technology is not the only factor driving the information society, it is a critical factor worthy of closer examination.

The current explosion of information technology is one of several great waves of development that have transformed the global economy since the late eighteenth century.[7] Each wave was driven by a unique set of technologies and institutions (see box 1.1). As they swept through society, these waves did more than just add new technologies and industries: instead, each one transformed the whole structure of the economy and many of the fundamental assumptions of society.

Box 1.1: Waves of Development

1771 – The Industrial Revolution (machines, factories, canals)
1829 – Age of steam, coal, iron, and railways
1875 – Age of steel and heavy engineering (electrical, chemical, civil, naval)
1920 – Age of internal combustion and the assembly line
1971 – Age of information and communications technology

Chart based on the concepts of Carlota Perez, see, for example, http://www.carlotaperez.org/pubs.

For example, starting in the late 1770s machines, factories, and canals shaped the Industrial Revolution. The "age of steam and coal" revolutionized transportation, shrinking distances and opening up new frontiers in trade and human migration. The "age of steel" began the transformation of cities into their modern form, as well as fundamentally changing the nature of warfare and with it the structure of geopolitics. At the turn of the twentieth century, the rise of automobiles, petrochemicals, and mass production completely transformed our economy and our society.

Today we are in the midst of the age of information and communications technology. This shift is different from those that have come before, not least because information is fundamentally different from physical resources. This requires us to rethink many concepts we take for granted. For instance:[8]

1. Information is *expandable*: It expands as it is used.
2. Information is *not resource hungry*: Producing and distributing information requires very little in the way of energy and other physical or biological resources.
3. Information is *substitutable*: It can and increasingly does replace capital, labour, and physical materials.
4. Information is *transportable*: It moves at close to the speed of light.

5. Information is *diffusive*: Information wants to be free; it leaks universally, pervasively, and continuously. Monopolizing information is very nearly a contradiction in terms.
6. Information is *shareable*: If I sell you my automobile, you have it and I don't. But if I sell you an idea or give you a fact, we both have it.

The advent of the personal computer, the Internet, downloadable software (apps), mobile smart devices, cloud computing, and social networks has spawned new industries and transformed services. It has also changed the way we engage in traditional activities such as manufacturing and agriculture, leading to large improvements in productivity and reshaping financial markets from national to global. Nothing and no one has been untouched.

The pace of adoption of information and communications technology is breathtaking. The Internet, which served less than 1 per cent of the world's population in 1995, now reaches more than 40 per cent: 3.2 billion users at the end of 2015 with more coming online every day.[9] Mobile Internet access using smart devices is exploding, from zero in 2007 to over 1 billion in 2012, to 1.75 billion in 2014[10] (see figure 1.1). This is a global dynamic, and it favours those who comprehend the nature of the change and can harness its possibilities. A new set of global companies has emerged, including Apple, Google, Amazon, Facebook, and Alibaba, with many smaller companies bidding to join them. This situation has fostered the development of new business models and possibilities for change.

These changes are not without costs. Techno-economic revolutions undermine existing investments and expectations and change the economics of industries. They can lead to unemployment, shuttered businesses, and rising tension between "winners" and "losers." They challenge those who are slow to adapt or who cannot easily change behaviours and habits.

Like the printing press, electricity, and the steam engine, the Internet – especially the mobile Internet – is a drastic innovation[11] that is causing discontinuities not only at the industry level but also at the level of entire economies. It has already changed the

Figure 1.1: Internet and Mobile Users, 1994–2014*

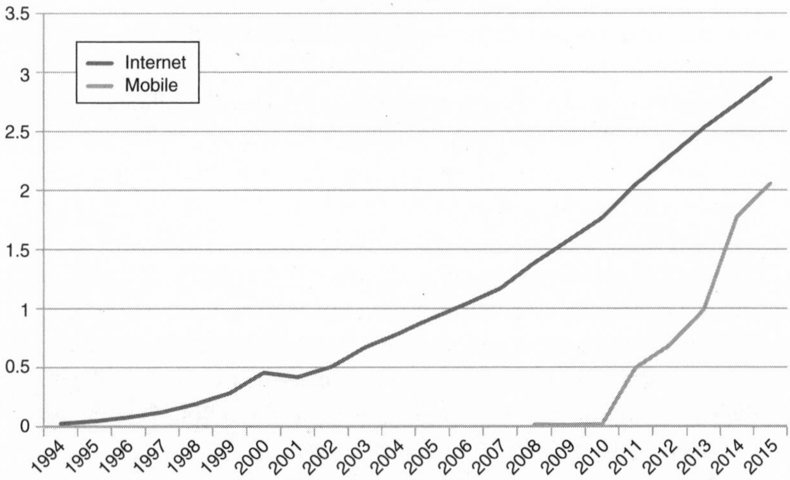

*as of July 2014

Sources: http://www.emarketer.com/Article/Worldwide-Smartphone-Usage-
Grow-25-2014/1010920
http://www.internetlivestats.com/internet-users/#trend

music, movie, newspaper, book publishing, and travel industries, and it is beginning to disrupt other service industries, including retail, health care, education, and finance (see box 1.2).

Box 1.2: Mobile Operating Systems

In July 2007 Apple launched the iPhone. While it offers many impressive features (multi-touch, Siri navigation, retina display, remarkable ease of use) its most impressive feature is the iOS operating system that brought us apps. Prior to the launch of the iPhone we had never heard of apps, and yet today they are pervasive.

- In June 2014 there were 1.2 million apps for Apple and 1.3 million for Google Play Store (formerly Android Market).
- More than 75 billion Apple apps and 80 billion Google Play apps have been downloaded as of June 2014.[12]
- Worldwide apps revenue totalled more than U.S. $35 billion in 2014; it is expected to exceed U.S. $75 billion within three years.
- As of June 2014, there were 800 million iTunes account holders with active credit cards on file.

From its humble start as a place to download music or TV episodes, iTunes became the core delivery platform for a whole new category of software and user experiences. Suddenly, consumers had access to products and services any place, any time, at the tips of their fingers. With the introduction of Apple Pay in September 2014, they are also able to engage in financial transactions.

Source: http://techcrunch.com/2013/09/19/gartner-102b-app-store-downloads-globally-in-2013-26b-in-sales-17-from-in-app-purchases/

These changes are happening globally.[13] One area that is being fundamentally transformed by information and communications technology and the information society is payments.

Impact on the Payments Ecosystem

The history of the Canadian payments system (CPS) has been one of thoughtful and gradual adaptation. Over the past decade, the CPS has carefully considered possible innovations and worked to ensure that they are smoothly implemented.[14]

It is easy to see why mobile smart technology is relevant to payments. Many banks offer apps that allow consumers online access to their accounts, and over the past decade those using online banking have increased from 8 per cent of Canadians to 77 per cent. Near-field communications (NFC) chips that enable contactless "tap" payments will soon be standard, and about half of all point of sale (POS) terminals now include this feature. Going to the

movies and buying a coffee can now be done "on the phone" using
Starbucks and Cineplex apps.

But true mobile payments in Canada are only in their infancy.
While consumers can transfer money using their handheld devices, the actual routing of payments from one account to another remains the same slow process as before, often taking two or three
business days.[15] The discrepancy between the promise of immediate payment offered by a handheld app and the actuality is mis-
leading and frustrating for the average consumer, who believes
immediate payment is a touch away. Until we are able to upgrade
what happens behind the screen, the full potential of this payment
revolution remains elusive.

Growth in mobile payments is taking place all over the globe
and at an ever-increasing rate. Some of the most significant changes include moves to phase out and replace cheques,[16] a decline in
the use of plastic cards, the rise of online banking, the rapid development of mobile payments options, and many more. Consumers
in Kenya, Afghanistan, Japan, and South Korea have been making
phone payments for years (see box 1.3 for some examples).

Box 1.3: Worldwide Development of Mobile Payments

The first generation of mobile payments was designed in a more or less
piecemeal fashion. Each system was designed in response to particular
problems in the market where it was deployed.

In *Kenya*, the key driver was lack of access to bank accounts. Wireless carrier Vodafone invested in M-PESA, allowing people to use
low-functionality phones to send money transfers or make payments
anywhere, bypassing the banks. Since M-PESA launched in Kenya in
2007, the need for cash has been reduced by 40 per cent. In 2012, over
25 per cent of the economy was supported by M-PESA. Vodafone has
since copied the model into other markets, including Tanzania and
Afghanistan.

In *Japan*, the development of smart cards was driven by public transportation and the growing inconvenience of collecting cash fares from
commuters in Tokyo and Osaka. To address this problem, Japanese

wireless carrier NTT DoCoMo used its dominant market share to de-velop a portable contactless solution and encourage its adoption.

In the *Netherlands*, the three largest wireless carriers formed a joint ven-ture with the three largest banks to develop a mobile payments platform.

In 2010 the *United States*-based Isis (now Softcard), a joint venture representing wireless carriers Verizon, AT&T, and T-Mobile, announced its intention to offer mobile payments on the rails of the Discover Card, bypassing mainstream financial institutions. This venture arose after efforts among banks and wireless carriers had failed to resolve who owns the customer relationship. Recently Softcard has indicated plans to open itself to all networks and banks.

Google, Apple, Amazon, Facebook, PayPal, and AliPay have all made inroads into mobile payments. And their ambitions reach beyond simply facilitating transactions: more and more these in-novators are seeking to revolutionize the entire shopping experi-ence, moving beyond e-payments to e-commerce.[17] As customers begin to demand greater convenience and a more streamlined and personalized experience, new services are being developed to meet that need. Some apps note the time and the user's location and generate coupons and loyalty points, offering instantaneous downloads for nearby stores or services. Others aim to archive transactions so that consumers have immediate access to warran-ties, returns, and servicing. For companies like Apple, Google, and PayPal, mobile payments are the key to a much richer store of in-formation: the point of sale is the moment that crystallizes a myri-ad of data (where consumers go, what they look at, what sort of price checking and comparison shopping takes place, which cou-pons and special offers they respond to) into useful information. At the same time, these companies are working to improve the privacy and security of customers' data – for example, using stron-ger authentication, such as thumb-print recognition, global posi-tioning, and tokenization.

The expansion of the mobile universe does not stop with e-commerce, banks, and merchants; our social and political lives are being swept up in the information revolution. The mobile ecosystem soon promises to incorporate everything from driver's licences, health cards, and library records to purchase histories and frequent-flyer accounts. Multi-industry partnerships are springing up that seek to capture and leverage all this information. As ever more people and sectors are incorporated into this developing eco-system, the need for common standards and practices grows ever more pressing.

Leadership and Governance Are Lagging Behind

In this context, practices of leadership and governance are strug-gling to keep up. This is becoming especially clear in the case of payments systems, riding as they do at the leading edge of the emer-gence of a digital economy.

In this complex, interconnected, and rapidly changing world, where boundaries between organizations, industries, disciplines, sectors, and political jurisdictions are rapidly shifting, the very na-ture of leadership and governance must likewise transform. The likely impact of the information age on our systems of governance was articulated thirty years ago, in a prescient work by Harlan Cleveland. His insight, formulated well before the mass introduc-tion of the Internet, is worth quoting at length:

> Knowledge is power ... So the wider the spread of knowledge, the more power gets diffused. For the most part individuals and corporations and governments don't have a choice about this; it is the ineluctable consequence of creating – through education – societies with millions of knowledgeable people. More and more work gets done by horizontal process – or it doesn't get done. More and more decisions are made with wider and wider consultation – or they don't "stick." A revolution in the technology of organization – the twilight of hierarchy – is already well under way.
>
> In the old days when only a few people were well educated and "in the know," leadership of the uninformed was likely to be organized in vertical structures of command and control. Leadership of the informed is different: it results in the necessary action only if exercised mainly

by persuasion, bringing into consultation those who are going to have to do something to make the decision a decision. *In an information-rich polity, the very definition of control changes. Very large numbers of people empowered by knowledge assert the right or feel the obligation to "make policy."* Decision-making proceeds not by "recommendations up, orders down," but by development of a shared sense of direction among those who must form the parade if there is going to be a parade.

"Planning" cannot be done by a few leaders, or by even the brightest whiz-kids immured in a systems analysis unit or a planning staff. Real-life "planning" is the dynamic improvisation by the many on a general sense of direction – announced by the few, but only after genuine consultation with those who will have to improvise on it. Participation and public feedback become conditions precedent to decisions that stick. (Emphasis added.)[18]

Cleveland describes a deep-rooted cultural shift that has since been amplified and accelerated by technological change. As our information society distributes information ever more broadly, the very definition of control – of governance – must change to become more distributed, more inclusive, and more dialogue-based. Without such a change, we will develop policies that are ineffective and badly suited to the demands of the age – policies that will not "stick."

Every major wave of development reshapes its society and challenges existing models of governance. As it sweeps through a society, the wave upends many of the shared mental maps and models we use to make sense of the world, to communicate and work together, and to organize and govern ourselves. We are seeing the impact today: our old maps no longer correspond well to the world of our experience. Practitioners in many fields have begun a search for new ones, and for more effective ways of leading and governing in this new context.

The search for new maps was central to the establishment and work of the Payments Task Force. In the next chapter, we introduce the task force and describe how it used engagement and dialogue as the starting point for developing more effective ways to lead and govern Canada's payments system in the information age.

chapter two

Engagement and Dialogue

The Payments Task Force

The Task Force on the Payments System Review (or "Payments Task Force") was established by Canada's Minister of Finance in June 2010 (the first step in the catalytic governance model). It was tasked with a fourfold mandate: to review the safety, soundness, and efficiency of the payments system; to assess whether the system permits sufficient innovation and competition; to determine whether businesses and consumers are being well served by payments system providers; and to determine whether current oversight mechanisms remain appropriate in the changing payments landscape. The broad aim of the Payments Task Force was to ensure that the framework supporting the payments system remains effective in light of new participants and innovations, and to make Canada's payments system a leader and an example for the rest of the world to follow. The task force report to the Minister of Finance was released to the public in March 2012.

In earlier, less turbulent times, task forces reviewing the payments system had been composed mostly of financial services industry insiders. Such an approach made sense when Canada's payments system had been the protected domain of financial institutions; however, in light of the current wave of global revolutionary change something different was required. Understanding the need for a broader approach this time around, the Minister of Finance (on the advice of the task force chair) selected a diverse group of task force members with a wide range of relevant experience and expertise. This group, balanced in terms of gender, age, and geographical location, was chosen for its expertise in economics, law, finance, technology, marketing, and banking. It was designed to move beyond the usual suspects of financial institutions and networks and ensure a stronger voice for users.

Getting Started

The Payments Task Force began its work in a fairly traditional manner, by undertaking and commissioning intensive research. From the outset, however, it attempted to make this process more open, inclusive, and collaborative than ever before in this field. It launched a first-ever online consultation, asking stakeholders and the general public to identify payments issues they found pressing; these conversations were held in open Internet forums, allowing participants to interact not only with the task force but also with each other. The open invitation to participate resulted in submissions from concerned citizens, banks, associations, and new entrants to the payments system.

The task force also commissioned several reports and made them available for public review. Deloitte Canada prepared a comprehensive analysis, *The Canadian Payments Landscape*, which was made available online for public comment and revision. In addition, the task force commissioned a report from consumer groups detailing their concerns and frustrations with the payments system. This report was a joint effort of many consumer groups and gave details of hundreds of consumer issues with payments. This report, too, was made available for public review on the task force website.

In addition to commissioning these reports, the task force conducted extensive domestic and international research, and made the results available online. This research included analysing payment innovations (including mobile payments and virtual currencies) and integrated electronic invoicing and payment solutions, as well as weighing the promise and challenge of digital identification and authentication. The task force also hired a former executive from the wireless carrier and mobile payments industry to advise on emerging trends in payments and security.

In its international research, the task force interviewed international payments experts and studied payments systems around the globe, including in Australia, Brazil, the Single European Payments Area (SEPA), New Zealand, South Africa, the United Kingdom, and the United States.[1] It assessed Canada's patchwork of laws and codes affecting payments, and compared them to other governance models around the world.

At its initial meeting on 28 June 2010, the task force established the goals and aspirations that would guide its work and, ultimately, its recommendations. Its primary goal was to develop and implement a framework that would enable Canada to become a world leader in payments by 2020. More specifically, it sought to create a low-cost Canadian online payments network that is easy to use, provides real-time information to all participants, and is accessible to all users. The system would need to include a clearly defined transition path from existing legacy systems to new digital systems, as well as cost-efficient solutions to concerns about security, safety, and privacy.

The task force also needed to find ways of helping Canadians understand and embrace the new technology and to ensure that stakeholders were heard and their concerns were addressed. Most importantly, the new system needed to redefine the industry around payments – wherever and however they take place – rather than around the specific players, such as banks, that had been the focus in the past.

Building on the issues raised by stakeholders, its own independent research, and its overarching objectives, the task force identified four fundamental challenges that had to be addressed for Canada to become a leader in payments.

1. **Increase fairness in credit and debit card networks.** The cost to merchants of accepting credit cards had risen dramatically in the previous few years. Not only did merchants have to adopt costly new technology and standards, they also had to accommodate popular loyalty and reward programs offered by card issuers. In addition, Visa and MasterCard had introduced surcharges that created an opportunity for merchant acquirers – the intermediaries that connect merchants to payment networks – to increase their fees as well.

2. **Update Canada's regulatory and governance structure.** The patchwork of legislation governing payments in Canada was incapable of meeting the challenges that lay ahead. And those rules were applied inconsistently, creating uncertainty that hampered innovation and competition.

3. **Improve online authentication, security, and privacy.** The fact that online payments require digital identification and authentication raises a host of security and privacy issues. With the emerging digital environment rapidly expanding to include new products and services, such as mobile applications and NFC-enabled tap-to-pay cards and phones, better ways are needed to identify and authenticate payers and payees over the Internet, in order to address the security and privacy issues presented by online commerce.

4. **Manage the transition to a digital economy.** Most payments will soon move online, but Canada still relies on paper cheques designed for a pre-connected computer era. Government and industry need to prepare together to ensure a smooth and successful transition to a digital economy.

During the three-month start-up phase (June to September 2010), the task force held hundreds of meetings with stakeholders, laying the foundation for ongoing engagement and collaboration in the effort to come.

Engaging Stakeholders

From the outset the Payments Task Force operated on the assumption that while it did not have "the answer," it could find better ways forward through a process of engaging stakeholders in dialogue (the second step in the catalytic governance model).

In the past, and across a wide range of issues, the authors have found that this assumption ("We do not have the answer") is essential for effective engagement and productive dialogue. But this is a difficult assumption to uphold in a culture that emphasizes expertise: part of the challenge of engagement is to create an environment of collaboration and mutual respect that recognizes that every stakeholder holds a piece of the answer. In such an environment, multiple perspectives and differing viewpoints become strengths rather than challenges or signs of weakness. In its work, the task force adopted several strategies to promote stakeholder engagement: some were familiar, like consultation and one-on-one meetings; others – like the Payments Roundtable – were truly transformative.

Consultation

The task force also sought the input of small and medium-sized businesses at face-to-face consultations with six groups of between twenty and thirty business leaders. These discussions – held in Halifax, Montreal, Toronto, Winnipeg, Calgary, and Vancouver – gave the task force an invaluable opportunity to hear from primary users of the payments system, many of whom spoke directly and with passion. In addition, the task force held hundreds of face-to-face consultations with business leaders representing more than seventy-five different organizations, each representing another opportunity to dig deeper and understand payment issues better.

Social Media

The Payments Task Force also used the Internet and social media to seek input from a broader cross-section of the public. The task force asked that all submissions be posted on its website. This meant that the submissions were open and available to everyone at the same time. All of the research conducted, the submissions received, and the scenarios developed were published on the task force website in a manner that facilitated comments and conversation. As the task force moved forward, a video illustrating different options for the future and their implications for consumers and small businesses was created and launched, with social media support, to encourage a broader discussion of payments issues. These efforts met with mixed success. Making documents accessible online meant they were far more widely distributed than might otherwise have been the case: key task force documents were downloaded more than 60,000 times each. However, efforts to engage a wider audience in

two-way conversation were not as successful as had been hoped –
in part because of a security breach when hackers broke into
Canadian government websites, and in part because of the task
force's limited experience with using social media. In spite of this
rocky start, it was clear that online engagement has a great deal of
potential to facilitate public discussions of this kind. Finding effective means of doing so will be crucial in future efforts to develop a
more inclusive and dialogue-based process of governance. The
work of the task force in engaging broader publics both online and
in other ways was an important step forward relative to what had
been done before; but much more remains to be done in this area.

The Roundtable

The most dramatic and revolutionary stakeholder engagement
strategy used by the task force was the Payments Roundtable,
created to engage current and future players in the payments ecosystem. This critical innovation brought together a diverse group
of some forty very senior practitioners (including CEOs and other leaders), with roughly equal numbers drawn from each of the
following groups:

- *The incumbents*, or current operators of the payments system.
  These included the networks (Visa, MasterCard, Interac, and
  the Canadian Payments Association), the Bank of Canada, all
  six large Canadian banks, the credit unions, and other financial
  institutions;
- *New entrants*. These included all three large wireless carriers,
  major retailers, payments entrepreneurs, loyalty programs, and
  technology companies; and
- *Users of the system*. These included corporations, small and
  medium-sized businesses, and retail and consumer organizations.
  All seven members of the Payments Task Force were included
  as members of the Roundtable as part of this "user" cohort.

The members of the Roundtable were selected to be a microcosm
of the emerging payments ecosystem. The key questions were:

"Which viewpoints need to be at the table?" and "Who can speak effectively from each perspective?" During selection of the members, these questions were repeated several times to identify which perspectives were missing and to fill those gaps. The government (both officials and the Minister of Finance) worked actively with the task force chair to determine which voices needed to be at the table. For example, the Minister emphasized the need to include a strong contingent of users of the system. The Minister also reviewed the proposed membership and roundtable process before authorizing it to proceed. As individuals, members of the Roundtable were selected who would be open to dialogue, who could speak and participate in their own right rather than just as representatives of groups or organizations, who could work together as peers, and who would be in a position to act on the results.

The original budget for the task force did not include the funds needed for the Roundtable, so members were asked to help cover the costs on a sliding scale according to their resources. Incumbents and larger new entrants were each asked to pay an equal share, while smaller organizations among the new entrants were asked to pay half that amount. Organizations representing payment system users (consumers, small business, etc.) were asked to pay only the cost of their own travel and accommodation to participate. One benefit of this approach was that Roundtable members had a stronger sense of shared ownership and of having some "skin in the game."

In addition to engaging the Roundtable itself, the task force also brought together a wider group of stakeholders to reflect on the Roundtable's work near the end of the Roundtable process. This larger group of stakeholders was invited to work through the preliminary scenarios produced by the Roundtable, to engage in dialogue with Roundtable members, and to suggest improvements.

Throughout the process the task force used many different approaches and invested considerable effort to engage an ever-widening range of stakeholders. The process resembled ripples spreading outward from a pebble tossed into a pond. The initial ripple began with the task force, then expanded to the Roundtable, to the wider group of stakeholders who met with the Roundtable, to the hundreds engaged in the working and advisory groups, and then to a range of publics engaged through meetings with the task force, formal submissions, and social media (see box 2.1).

Box 2.1: Widening Circles of Engagement

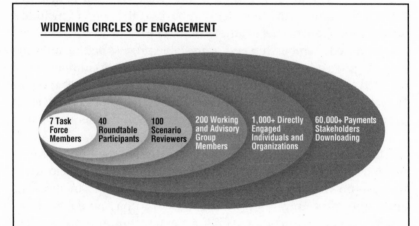

WIDENING CIRCLES OF ENGAGEMENT

7 Task Force Members — 40 Roundtable Participants — 100 Scenario Reviewers — 200 Working and Advisory Group Members — 1,000+ Directly Engaged Individuals and Organizations — 60,000+ Payments Stakeholders Downloading

7 Task Force Members

Members were appointed by the Minister of Finance and the task force was provided with $5 million of funding to address the challenges defined in its mandate.

40 Roundtable Participants

Very senior practitioners (including CEOs and other leaders) were invited to participate because they represented one of three key stakeholder groups: incumbents, new entrants, and users of the Canadian payments system. They represented a microcosm of the emerging payments ecosystem. (The Roundtable participants are listed at the beginning of this volume.[2])

100 (including the Roundtable) Scenario Reviewers

Senior executives were recruited from a wide range of sectors, including government, consumer groups, banking and other financial services, small and large retailers, manufacturing, and communications and technology companies. They were asked to review the scenarios and offer suggestions for improvement.

200 Working and Advisory Group Members

Key individuals engaged in five working groups and three advisory groups were tasked with developing initiatives to implement the desired vision of the Canadian payments system.

1,000+ Individual Contributors

Individuals and organizations were involved through meetings with the task force, formal submissions, and online comments. Although not formally working with the task force, many of these individuals were engaged in the widening discourse about the Canadian payments industry.

60,000+ Payments Stakeholders

Key individual documents downloaded included *The Payments Landscape; Scenarios for the Future of the Canadian Payments System; The Way We Pay; Going Digital;* and the task force's final report, *Moving Canada into the Digital Age.* Also, conference attendees included participants in the CPA and TMAC conferences in June 2012 and in several "mobile payments" conferences throughout the year.

Overall, the goal of this engagement phase was to redefine and broaden the boundaries of the payments community. To bring about this more inclusive community, the task force reached out to traditional interests, new players, and users to get them to join. As they engaged these stakeholders the task force emphasized that they would be doing things differently than in the past: this task force process would be open, transparent, and highly collaborative. There would be no lobbying behind closed doors. Rather than simply advocating and hoping to be heard, participants would work together to craft solutions. And this payments review process would be forward looking: rather than trying to protect the status quo and postpone the inevitable, it would focus on making changes that would actively embrace the digital age.

The Payments Roundtable

Interviewing Roundtable Members

The Payments Roundtable played a central role in the work and learning process of the task force as well as in engaging stakeholders. The Roundtable process began well before its members convened as a group. In the two months before the Roundtable's first meeting, Ged Davis and Steven Rosell (along with their Viewpoint Learning colleague Daniel Coates) conducted interviews with twenty-one of its members, representing a cross-section of participants. The interviews asked respondents for their views about the payments system. What did they believe were its current positives and negatives? What might the Canadian payments system look like in the future? What would the "status quo" scenario look like? What would be their "ideal" scenario? What would be their "nightmare"? What alternative payment ecosystems exist today or could be visualized? What were the key uncertainties clouding the future, and what did they think were the potential obstacles to change?

These interviews provided an important starting point for understanding the many perspectives this diverse group of Roundtable members brought to the broader issues: how did these different individuals see the agenda that the Roundtable would need to address, and what language did they use to describe it? Just as important, by providing an opportunity to listen intently to each participant, the interviews set the stage for an ongoing dialogue process.

The interviews explored respondents' perceptions and anxieties through a series of open-ended questions and careful attention to the answers. Participant responses guided not only the further course of the interview but also fundamentally shaped the work of the Roundtable by helping to articulate the perimeters of the issue, identify key themes, and begin to establish a common language.

The interviews also identified important unknowns that Round-table members wanted to understand better – information that set the agenda for the expert panels at the first meeting.

The main themes raised by the interviews are shown in figure 2.1.

Most participant responses could be mapped onto two axes: Canadian/global and optimism/concern.

1. Themes that were predominantly Canadian are towards the top of this chart, and those dealing with other (or all) countries are towards the bottom.
2. Themes that were "optimistic" are towards the left of the chart, while those raising "concerns" are to the right.

The lighter ovals represent themes that focused on the Canadian payments system (CPS) today, while the darker ovals represent those that focused on the future of the CPS.

Figure 2.1: Perspectives on the Future of the Canadian Payments System

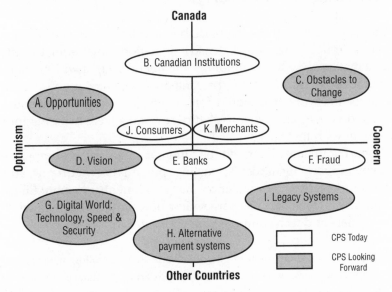

Canada

B. Canadian Institutions

C. Obstacles to Change

A. Opportunities

Optimism

J. Consumers   K. Merchants

Concern

D. Vision   E. Banks   F. Fraud

I. Legacy Systems

G. Digital World: Technology, Speed & Security

H. Alternative payment systems

CPS Today

CPS Looking Forward

Other Countries

Cross-cutting these themes were significant differences in participants' perspectives. In particular, throughout the process the Roundtable's work needed to take into account:

- the views of those who believed in the radical application of new technology versus those who preferred incremental change;
- the views of those who emphasized the need for dramatic innovation versus those who were more concerned about security risks;
- the views of those who supported current institutional arrangements versus those who believed in the need for a more open system;
- the differing views held by industry incumbents, existing/potential new entrants, and users of the system, as well as each group's assumptions, suspicions, and mistrust about the others.

Feeding Back Interview Findings

At its first workshop, the Roundtable heard a synopsis of the interview findings, including extensive quotations illustrating the different perspectives that Roundtable members brought with them to the process. These comments, presented without attribution, set the stage for the work that would follow by presenting, and to some degree defusing, the tensions that participants were bringing into the room with them.

Some comments illustrated the different views and assumptions held by industry incumbents, existing/potential new entrants, and users of the system. For instance, many comments illustrated how incumbent players such as banks view new entrants such as wireless carriers and tech companies, and vice versa:

> There's a whole body of regulations we banks have to follow when we accept customers, when we do transactions and compliance, and it's definitely not the same for [the new entrants]. Whenever a newcomer comes in, if they don't obey the same rules, for me it creates risks.

[As a mobile payments technology provider,] I am motivated because I'm a new entrant in the payment ecosystem and because there's more money in it for me. [The banks] are de-motivated because they believe if I enter, it will come out of their pocket. I don't believe that for a minute. I think there's more money to be made on all sorts of fronts, including by the banks, but they like it just the way it is.

I think there is an ongoing, below-the-surface struggle going on which I'll euphemistically call a "turf war" between various players. I don't think the banks anticipated that the [wireless carriers] would actually want to get into the transaction business.

The banks cannot do [wireless carrier] business. They are forbidden from doing that. But [wireless carriers] can come and play in the payments field.

Other comments demonstrated the mutual mistrust among different players in the system:

[I'm a banker, and] I don't think merchants are looking for a fair system, I think they are looking for a biased system.

EMV[3] is a project that will cost merchants millions of dollars. It doesn't help us [merchants]. Everyone may tell you about the security of EMV, but it's a product for the card issuers, for them to have less fraud. It's not my problem and it's not the merchants' problem either. But we've got a new mandate because it helps the card issuers.

In the Canadian market, because we have few banks, they tend to be omnipresent in all fields and control everything. The concentration of power within the Canadian banks is something that we have to take care of as Canadians.

The power of the banks! I laugh at the comment in many ways. What power?

Some comments focused on the opportunities presented by radical technological change while others focused on managing its risks.

The Internet changes everything; it is the number one driver. Scope, speed, and implications of the digital revolution and the diminishing boundary between the real and virtual world.

I see technology like contactless and mobile really gaining hold over the next couple of years among consumer groups. I see a lot of demand for that, particularly from the youth segment.

Ten years from now, I don't think our customers are all going to say, "I want to do everything electronically."

If we don't move forward, I think that as technology around us continues to accelerate, it will become even more noticeable that we're so far behind in this area.

You cannot change technology just because it's the new thing around town, because the cost to do that is tremendous.

Usually we [banks] are not ahead of the curve in terms of technology. We have safe technology, proven technology, and something that is very stable to handle our business.

Other comments highlighted the differences between those who supported current institutional arrangements and those who believed in the need for a more open system – a conversation that often turned on the cost of change versus the cost of *not* changing:

I don't see a huge wave [of innovation] coming and changing dramatically the way [the banks] do business. It has to be done slowly, surely, and it's the forces of the market that drive innovation. It should not come from government policy. It's the market that drives innovation, and it's the forces within that market.

[As a banker] I don't think there are a lot of negatives to not doing anything, so I am not a believer that there is a burning platform or a big problem to fix. However, having said that there's always room to make it better.

When I look at the rest of the world, I see lots of innovation all over the place. That's not happening in Canada. Why is that so? And I think part of the answer is the way the system is governed or, rather, not governed. It's a mess out there!

I think the pace of change will not be as rapid as it would have been had more entrepreneurial companies accessed market opportunities rather than slow-moving, risk-averse banks.

I wonder about some of these big banks because the best scenario for them seems to be no change. Change costs money and they make so much money on all these payment schemes and cards that they issue. Any future technology or future way of doing things seems to make them less money.

If we do nothing, the big [tech] guys will take over.

At the first Roundtable meeting, participants engaged with these quotes and the interview synopses and mapped out some of the patterns they saw at work – a process that did a great deal to establish a common language and a better understanding of the range of perspectives and concerns in the room. Having this feedback presented without attribution allowed participants to focus on the content rather than initially assessing each comment in terms of who was speaking or what sector the person represented. And seeing all these comments together allowed people to see their own concerns upheld even as other, competing concerns were articulated. Both represented important steps in defusing participants' initial mistrust and misunderstanding and helped to clear away many initial obstacles that would otherwise have got in the way of the work of the first meeting.

Overall, the interview process helped jump-start the Roundtable's work in two key ways. First it brought together a wide range of voices and perspectives on a complex issue. And second, the interview process itself, by modelling attentive listening and constructive testing of assumptions, provided a valuable demonstration of what dialogue is and how it can work in addressing complex problems.

Using Dialogue

Dialogue excels as a tool for bridging diverse perspectives in this way, and its use was fundamental to the work of the task force and the Roundtable. The specific dialogue process used by the task force and described here was developed by Steven Rosell, Daniel Yankelovich, and their colleagues at Viewpoint Learning, who had applied it previously to a wide range of issues in the United States and Canada, including fiscal policy, health care, education, climate change, and sustainability.[4]

Dialogue is a powerful method groups can use to build trust and create a shared language and framework – a shared mental map that enables those with different backgrounds, assumptions, and interests to work together. Such differences (along with associated misunderstanding and mistrust) were very evident in the initial interviews we conducted with members of the Roundtable as well as at its first meeting.

But this mutual mistrust changed as the Roundtable members worked together over many months, using dialogue to learn from each other and from outside experts. In this process, a sense of mutual trust and understanding, respect, and community grew among a group of leaders who previously had known each other mostly by reputation. One small sign of this occurred when the Roundtable broke into smaller groups. At first we needed to take great care to be sure that each group reflected the diversity of the full Roundtable, and so carefully pre-defined who would be in each small group. But very soon we were able to let Roundtable members join whichever small group they wished, and those groups would self-organize to be sure a wide range of perspectives were included.

The dialogue process allowed participants to explore others' perspectives and assumptions, understand them more deeply, and look for common ground. As described in chapters 3 and 4, participants worked together to frame and re-frame questions, embark on joint inquiry, and create shared agendas, stories, language, and meaning. Those who initially identified primarily as bankers, or tech executives, or telecom experts, or retailers gradually came to see themselves as part of a more inclusive payments *ecosystem or industry*, a concept that did not exist prior to the work of the task force and the Roundtable. For many, realizing the existence of a distinctive payments industry and their role in it was itself a new insight – a new mental map that the work of the task force and the Roundtable then developed further. In effect, the Roundtable became the catalyst for the payments ecosystem to become self-aware and then begin to define its possible path forward. The result was a powerful community engaged in a shared search for greater understanding and more effective approaches to organize, lead, and govern Canada's payments ecosystem in the information age.

At the end of their fourth and concluding workshop, Roundtable members reflected on the outcomes their dialogue had produced. Their expressed sense of community and a shared mental map, as well as collective ownership of the outcomes, is remarkable – especially when compared with the comments from the interviews that had been presented at the first Roundtable meeting. The following are quotes from Roundtable members at their fourth workshop.

> We did not have a common lexicon when we walked in here at the end of last year. We didn't really understand or agree about what the options were – but when we sat down we saw that there were a lot more commonalities in our thoughts and purposes than differences. I think when we first walked in the room we really were focusing on the differences as opposed to the commonalities that we see now.

> It's been a great process and great dialogue. Having been in this business for a while, the idea that this is a payments industry is a huge deal. This will make a tremendous difference to how we think, how we work, and how we interact as an industry. I see we've called it an ecosystem, and that gives some context to it.

> I think back to September when this started. There was a fair bit of scepticism and cynicism in the room, and people were curious as to where this was going to go. I heard a lot of comments at the water cooler as I wandered around. And the change [since then] is incredible to hear.

> This used to be an exclusive club. I think this process has demonstrated that it ought to be and has become an inclusive club. There has been

a lot of dialogue and trust developed, and the collaboration is a good working model.

I'm really encouraged to see the open dialogue with the retailers and the consumer groups. It's long overdue. I'm very encouraged that it's become a much more inclusive process and I think we're all learning that we can benefit as participants from that inclusiveness.

My observation from working both north and south of the border is that today politicians and lawyers are designing the payment systems in North America. And they are absolutely the worst ones to be doing it – the outcomes are crap for everybody. If we don't get this right, we won't reclaim this ground where collaboration between merchants, between acquirers, between banks and everyone else can find fruitful solutions. If we let lawyers and politicians do it, it just becomes winners and losers. And the consequences of that are not good for the public. You don't get an efficient or good payment system.

I'm also very encouraged that we in this room feel like we own this as opposed to feeling like it's something that's being done to us. That's not just semantics; it's truly a difference in outlook and level of engagement.

The Roundtable members' growing sense of authorship and commitment to their shared mental map also energized the work of the task force. Most Roundtable members volunteered to participate in the working groups established by the task force to develop specific initiatives to change the payments industry, guided by that mental map (see chapters 4 and 5).

The dialogue process begun in the Roundtable continued and deepened further through the work of the task force.

What Is Dialogue?

One important and distinctive element of dialogue is that it includes the emotional dimension: something our conventional cognitively oriented model of knowledge and learning tries to exclude. The dialogue model, however, recognizes that strong feelings are bound to arise when fundamental questions of values, world view, interests, and identity are at issue. We frequently rely on both facts and values when reaching our most important judgments, and this mixing is also characteristic of dialogue. Well-functioning boards of directors, cabinets, working groups, and citizen groups all take the emotional as well as the factual into account, and we saw this process at work in the task force and the Roundtable as well.

Three features separate dialogue from simple discussion and most other forms of talk. For true dialogue to take place, it is essential that participants suspend status differences and treat one another as peers, listen to one another with empathy, and bring assumptions to the surface in a non-judgmental way.

One good way to understand the nature of dialogue is to contrast it with debate or advocacy, which is the predominant mode of discourse in our society.[5] While debate is a win/lose proposition, dialogue seeks to expand the terms of discussion and explore new possibilities (see table 2.1).

Table 2.1 Debate versus Dialogue

Debate/Advocacy	Dialogue
Assuming there is one right answer	Assuming others have pieces of the answer
About winning	About finding common ground
Listening for flaws	Listening to understand
Defending assumptions	Exploring assumptions
Seeking your outcome	Discovering new possibilities

This is not to say that dialogue is good and debate is bad. The two modes of discourse are based on different assumptions and have different purposes. The fundamental purpose of a debate is to win, while the fundamental purpose of a dialogue is to learn and understand. You cannot "win" a dialogue, but it can be transformative.

Debate is an extremely valuable tool for clarifying differences and advancing a specific goal or agenda, and it is often entertaining. Dialogue, however, excels at uncovering hidden assumptions, raising new possibilities, and mapping out common ground. Both modes are needed in a complex and changing world.

Unfortunately, dialogue is too often left out in traditional approaches to governance and decision making. Those traditional approaches tend to be relatively simple – issues arise, key interests advocate for their preferred solution, and a decision gets made. This may work well enough when the issues and the possible responses are reasonably well understood, and where everyone involved shares similar assumptions, language, background, and culture. But in the information age this is less and less often the case. As with the future of the payments ecosystem, when the issues and possible responses are unclear, and people with very different beliefs, interests, values, or traditions must find common ground, an additional step is needed. That is where dialogue comes in (see figure 2.2).

Dialogue is the step we can take, *before* decisions are made, to uncover assumptions, broaden perspectives, build trust, and find common ground. It does not replace debate, negotiation, or decision making. It precedes them, creating the trust, shared framework, language, and expectations that are more likely to lead to a productive outcome.

Putting this into practice requires some basic ground rules (see box 2.2).

Box 2.2: Ground Rules for Dialogue

The purpose of dialogue is to understand and learn from one another. You cannot "win" a dialogue

1. All dialogue participants speak for themselves, not as representatives of groups or special interests.
2. Treat everyone in a dialogue as an equal: leave role, status, and stereotypes at the door.
3. Listen with empathy to the views of others.
4. Be open and listen to others even (especially) when you disagree; resist the temptation to rush to judgment.
5. Search for assumptions (especially your own).
6. Look for common ground.
7. All points of view deserve respect, and all will be recorded (without attribution).

Figure 2.2: Dialogue and Decision Making: Adding the Missing Step

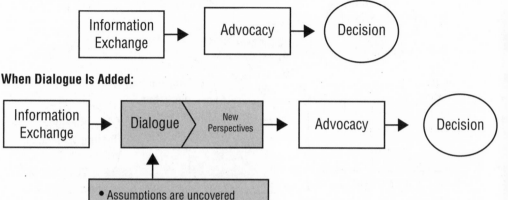

Roundtable members were briefed on the dialogue approach at their first workshop, and they quickly adopted these ground rules as their own. The dialogue process became an essential part of the culture of the group and was largely self-policing – in fact, when Roundtable members spotted a departure from these ground rules they would call it out (usually with some humour) and it would be corrected. We have seen many different types of groups quickly embrace dialogue in this way and incorporate it into their standard procedures; it is a form of discourse that most find very appealing, once barriers to its use are relaxed.

Designing the Roundtable Process

The Roundtable process was designed to be a series of steps, each building on the ones before (see figure 2.3).[6]

The learning process began with the in-depth interviews of individual Roundtable members described above, which set the stage for dialogue by outlining the perspectives and priorities of diverse participants and beginning to shape a common language and

Figure 2.3: The Canadian Payments System Roundtable Process

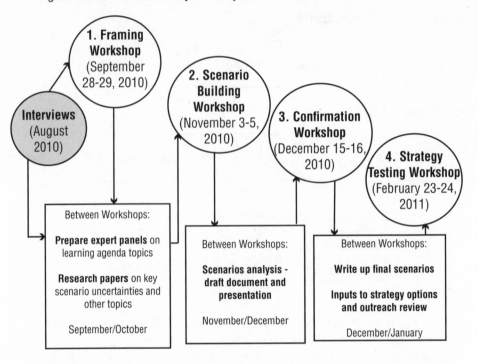

framework for their work together. From this starting point, the process then built through four subsequent workshops, which are described more fully in chapters 3 and 4.

First, the *Framing Workshop* introduced participants to each other and briefed them on the dialogue and scenario process. Participants heard the results of the interviews, as well as from two panels of outside experts (selected based on findings from the interviews and initial research). Based on these inputs, participants set a "Learning Agenda" of the issues relevant to the future of the Canadian payments system (CPS), laying the groundwork for the later work of constructing scenarios for the future of the CPS.

The *Scenario Building Workshop* began with additional panels of outside experts suggested by the participants' Learning Agenda.

The Roundtable then constructed the scenarios, a process that continued in the weeks between this workshop and the next one.

Next, the *Confirmation Workshop* was devoted to finalizing the scenarios. Roundtable members presented the scenarios to a larger group of invited stakeholders, who then worked with Roundtable members to challenge, improve, and develop them further. This larger group of stakeholders not only provided input into the evolving scenarios; in the process they also gained a much better understanding of changes occurring in the payments ecosystem, which they later told us changed their perceptions and actions going forward.

Last, in the *Strategy Testing Workshop*, participants put the finalized scenarios into practice, using them to "wind-tunnel" test several policy options being considered by the task force. They concluded the workshop with a discussion of next steps and plans for continued action.

An important part of the Roundtable process took place between workshops, when participants and organizers conducted research, consolidated conclusions from previous meetings, selected and briefed outside experts, and wrote up scenarios. Participants also often met with each other between sessions, getting to know each other better and strengthening their collaboration. In addition, after each workshop a detailed summary of that session was prepared and circulated to all members, and these summaries became an important part of the Roundtable's shared memory.

The meeting spaces for the workshops were carefully designed to support the process. For example, we generally met in a single large room furnished with wheeled armchairs and no tables. This not only facilitated the forming and reforming of groups as the process unfolded (it was not unusual to see participants scooting from one group to another on their chairs), it also helped encourage closer collaboration by eliminating tables and other barriers that could divide participants both physically and psychologically. We worked to minimize distractions: meeting rooms were placed far from other groups' gatherings, and healthy snacks and beverages were always available in the room to help reduce the need to break away from the work of the group. We also used handheld wireless microphones during discussions: these served as a kind of "talking stick" (ensuring it was clear who had the floor), as well as providing a clear recording of what was said. These recordings were used to prepare detailed summaries of the conversation (without attribution to individuals), which were distributed to all participants after each workshop.[7]

Dialogue and Scenarios

Dialogue was one key to the Roundtable's success in creating shared mental maps and generating a more learning-based and inclusive process of leadership and governance.[8] The other key was the development of scenarios. Scenarios describe alternative plausible futures – each based on different assumptions – which we can use to broaden our perception, to try out different perspectives, and to develop a shared context and language for decision making. Because scenarios use multiple perspectives to explore problems rather than just extended and deeper analysis of a single viewpoint, they can help us to understand the significance of issues and events that we might otherwise dismiss as unimportant or might not see at all.

Scenario construction combined with effective dialogue is a proven way to tap into a diversity of views, challenge assumptions about what the future holds, explore uncertainties, reframe risks and opportunities, develop and stress-test strategies, and find common ground. The next chapters describe in more detail how we used scenario development in this effort, and how the work of the Roundtable unfolded.

chapter three

Exploring Perspectives and Building Scenarios

As summarized in chapter 2 (see figure 2.3) and elaborated below, the Payments Roundtable met four times, for two or three days each, over a period of six months. Over those six months the Roundtable invested a great deal of time and effort in understanding its members' perspectives, looking for common ground, exploring alternative futures, and creating a shared mental map and an associated sense of trust and community (using dialogue, scenarios, and smart process design), which catalysed much that followed. This is the third step in the catalytic governance model.

The Roundtable members' growing sense of authorship and commitment to the shared mental map they had created energized the work of the task force, and produced the core of a payments community with a shared vision of the future that they were willing, even eager, to co-create. This chapter describes the first three meetings of the Roundtable – the framing, scenario building, and confirmation workshops. The results of the fourth (strategy testing) workshop are summarized in chapter 4.

The Roundtable process was designed to achieve several important objectives including to:

- develop new insights and a shared understanding of the challenges facing the Canadian payments system;
- learn from one another and from leading outside authorities, in order to:
  - reframe the context for policy and strategy;

  – identify critical certainties and uncertainties;
  – define a set of possible alternative futures;
• consider changes needed to deal with each possible future;
• provide a better basis for serious, structured dialogue with
  stakeholders and the public; and
• explore different viewpoints in depth and look for common
  ground.

The workshops provided an unusual opportunity for real dialogue – Roundtable members were not only able but actively encouraged to be creative and "think outside the box," to break out
of the usual conversation and explore new territory.

To realize the above objectives and to provide a context for developing a new strategic direction for the Canadian payments system (CPS), the Roundtable began to build scenarios for the future
of the CPS. The scenario process used here was developed by Ged
Davis and had been applied previously with large groups in addressing issues including the future of energy,[1] environment,[2] and
health care.[3]

The Benefits of Building Scenarios Together

When organizations or individuals make decisions, they tend to
do so on the basis of their "mental map" of the future.[4] Just like
cartographic maps, our mental maps are constructions based on
and shaped by our culture, background, and life experiences. And
as with cartography, it is all too easy to accept our mental map as
the sole true representation of reality and to forget that other people's maps of the same territory may look quite different.

Until we compare our mental map and its embedded assumptions with those of others, we often don't know we have a map at
all – let alone what is distinctive about it, what it highlights, and
what it leaves out.

Rigorously analysed, plausible scenarios can challenge our current assumptions by presenting new interpretations of the maps
we already hold. Scenario thinking also improves our capacity to
manage uncertainty by showing us how much we *don't* know

when it comes to critical matters. This can be disconcerting: many human beings prefer to ignore uncertainty or erase it by simplifying their view of the world and their assumptions about how it works. However, these simplifications can betray us when we are trying to make specific decisions – especially about unfamiliar areas or at times of crisis. Scenario building requires us to frame our concerns precisely, and to focus on those issues that really matter, distinguishing between those which are relatively certain and likely to persist and those which are most uncertain and are likely to have the greatest impact on how the future turns out.

Effective planning for the future requires a comprehensive picture of the context in which we operate. This is difficult to achieve alone or in a small, homogeneous group. In general, our experience, training, current fashions, and familiar ideas strongly influence what we notice and how we interpret the world. These influences help us focus, but they can also create blind spots – whole areas we know nothing about – leaving us exposed to unanticipated developments. Expertise itself can, paradoxically, worsen these blind spots, as discipline-based research can create fragmented learning. We cannot make a coherent map of the future by ourselves – our blind spots impose limitations on our understanding – so we need to combine our knowledge and thinking with that of others who have different assumptions, mindsets, or interests.

Scenario building allows us to accomplish this in a number of complementary ways:

- It is a collaborative, conversation-based process that facilitates the interplay of a wide variety of ideas.
- It enables different fields of knowledge and ways of knowing to be combined.
- It reframes questions, prompting the generation of ideas across disciplines rather than going over old ground.
- It encourages the involvement of different perspectives on an issue or question.
- It does not demand consensus, but rather respects and accommodates differences, seeking only to define those differences clearly.

- It enables both qualitative and quantitative aspects to be incorporated by means of narratives and stories, so ideas are not excluded on the basis that they can't be measured.
- It can assemble several different versions of the future at the same time, so that participants can keep thinking of the future as full of possibilities.

Scenarios are not exact descriptions of future events – like early cartographic maps, they are guides for a territory that we have not yet seen. As described in box 3.1, they provide a framework for our explorations, raising our awareness and appreciation of uncertainty. They encourage us to broaden our perspective as we face the unknown, and they offer a structure and shared language for understanding events as they unfold. And by improving our understanding of the uncertainties we face, they can make change more manageable.[5]

Box 3.1. What Are Scenarios?

The practice of developing and using scenarios emerged as a way of providing collaborative foresight for decision takers that can underpin their strategy and policy in an uncertain world.

Scenarios use rigorous research and analysis to map out possible contrasting futures. They identify some significant events that will occur in the future, the main actors, and their motivations; and they convey how those future worlds function. Scenarios are a tool that can help us to better understand what the future might look like and the likely challenges of living in it.

Scenarios work in part because they force us to reflect on the assumptions we make about the world, address critical uncertainties, and widen our perspectives on what we need to consider in making successful strategy and policy.

One useful way of thinking about scenarios is to use the metaphor of exploration and map making. Like a set of maps describing different aspects of a new territory, scenarios provide us with a range of perspectives on what might happen, where pitfalls and roadblocks may occur, and where different paths may lead. *Creating* the map is as important as using it once it has been made. Building scenarios allows us to explore possible futures rigorously and systematically, and the act of making these maps can change how we see and understand the world.

Decision makers can use scenarios to think about aspects of the future that most worry them – or to discover which aspects *should* worry them – and to explore the ways these might unfold. Because there are many variables determining what will actually come to pass, scenario builders create several scenarios. These scenarios all address the same important questions and all include those aspects of the future that are likely to persist, but each one describes a different way in which the uncertain aspects of the future could play out.

As a basis for strategy development, scenarios are a method for considering potential implications of future events and possible responses to them. They provide their users with a common language for thinking and talking about current events, as well as a shared framework for exploring critical uncertainties and making more successful decisions.

The Framing Workshop

The Framing Workshop was the first major meeting of the Payments Roundtable and the start of the scenario-building process. At the outset of the Framing Workshop, all Roundtable members were asked to identify *one* aspect of the future of the Canadian payments system that they saw as most important or worrying. The range and variety of views reflected the diversity of participant priorities and perspectives. Some focused on relatively technical issues: data security, fraud, identity theft, or authentication. Some emphasized ensuring equity and equal access across all segments of Canadian society. Others were concerned with Canada's international competitiveness: not only how to keep from being left behind but how to become a leader on the world payments stage. Many participants expressed concern about the pace of change and how to manage it. Would consumers be driving that change or dragged along by it? What sort of new systems would be needed to support innovation that is fast but not *too* fast? Most centrally of all: What kind of governance systems would be needed? And what is the right balance between a dynamic free market and protective regulation? In the words of one participant, "How do we herd this bunch of tigers in a way that is almost fair to almost everybody?"

The Framing Workshop then reviewed the results of the interviews described in chapter 2. This was followed by presentations from two expert panels on critical topic areas that had been identified in those interviews.

Panel 1: Technology and the Business Landscape

The first panel highlighted how advanced technology and its applications are remaking the business landscape, with profound implications for payments. The first speaker, John Seely Brown,[6] Independent Co-chair of the Deloitte Center for the Edge and former long-time head of Xerox PARC, argued that exponential advances in computation, storage, and bandwidth, an explosion of information, and the growing importance of network effects and cloud solutions have created a "new normal" – an era of constant disequilibrium that Seely Brown predicted will transform IT, disrupt many industries, and change the way business – especially in terms of payments – is conducted.[7]

The second speaker, MIT Media Lab's Pranav Mistry (now Global Vice-president of Research at Samsung), demonstrated some of the newer frontiers of personal technology with a presentation of his prototype "SixthSense"[8] wearable gestural interface.[9] The implications for the payments system were clear: if someone can take a picture by holding her fingers out in a "framing" gesture and send that picture to a friend with a few simple movements, she will expect similar simplicity, accessibility, and security when it comes to making a purchase or transferring money between bank accounts.

This panel shook many Roundtable members out of their comfort zone. Many were astonished by the magnitude, speed, and pervasiveness of technological change the presenters described. They saw a world where new technologies could no longer be considered as mere tools: they were change agents with the potential to drive the development of organizations, industries, or even societies. Many of those present (especially the bankers) had walked in assuming that technological changes could be absorbed or managed without broad-based and dramatic action. That assumption was now called seriously into question.

Panel 2: Payments Systems around the World

The second panel discussed payments systems around the world. First, Philip Bruno, a leader of the payments practice at McKinsey and Company, provided an overview of the broad diversity of international payments systems and their varying customer needs, competitive dynamics, infrastructure, and regulation. Compared to other countries, he noted that Canada lags significantly in B2B, e-invoicing, contactless prepaid cards, and clearing and settlement infrastructure – and that Canada also lacks many of the drivers that would encourage innovation in these and other areas.

Next, Kristopher Haag of the U.S. Department of Defense described the effort to build a new retail payments system in postwar Iraq as an example of the way that a developing country can leapfrog past a developed country. This integrated solution brings together multiple banks and wireless carriers in a more streamlined and interoperable system.[10]

In the dialogue that followed this panel, Roundtable members, who had come in with a belief that Canada was a global leader in payments,[11] expressed deep surprise at the analysis showing that Canada's payments system is lagging behind those of other countries, especially when it comes to mobile payments, electronic invoicing, and B2B payments. They were also struck by the degree to which developing countries, without an installed base, have the potential to build state-of-the-art payments systems that can leapfrog over the stable legacy systems found in developed countries.

Uncertainties and Initial Storylines

After the panel presentations, Roundtable participants embarked on one of the core tasks of the scenario-building process: identifying the uncertainties that would shape the future as it unfolded. These uncertainties – things that turn out one way in one scenario and a different way in another scenario – frame and differentiate possible futures.

In this Framing Workshop participants took the first steps on that journey. Based on participants' initial concerns, the report on the interviews, the first two panels, and dialogue with one another, the Roundtable identified a preliminary list of the uncertainties that they felt would shape the Canadian payments system over the next ten years.[12] Working first in small groups and then in a plenary session, Roundtable members arrived at the following list:

- **Technology and Innovation:** What will be the pace, scope, and nature of technological innovation?
- **Security, Authentication, and Privacy:** How will we address growing security and privacy concerns?
- **Consumer and Business Adoption:** How rapidly will new information technologies and social networking be adopted? How much resistance will there be? How will changing demography and consumer needs shape the requirements that a payments system will need to meet?
- **Regulation:** What will be the timing, nature, and extent of new regulation of the CPS?
- **Industry Ecosystem:** How collaborative or fragmented will the payments industry be? What will happen in each zone of the industry ecosystem: what will be the source of leadership; how much cooperation will there be among key players; and what will be the impact on economics and business models? Who will pay for changes in the Canadian payments system, and who will benefit from them?
- **Global Developments:** How will changes in payments and regulation outside of Canada affect the Canadian payments system?

These uncertainties formed the kernel of a growing list that would develop through the panels and discussions at the next workshop, culminating in a set of focal questions that would guide the construction of the scenarios.

The Roundtable then divided into four smaller groups to build preliminary storylines about the future of the Canadian payments system, using these key uncertainties as their starting points. Each group was asked to select two key uncertainties and then to develop storylines based on the different possible resolutions of those uncertainties.

This step had a twofold purpose. First, by working with a preliminary set of uncertainties to imagine storylines, Roundtable members moved from seeing the future not as a narrow set of probable outcomes but as a branching set of possibilities – each pair of uncertainties mapped into four possible futures, so among them the four small groups of participants created a total of sixteen futures they could "try on" and test. In addition the exercise allowed Roundtable members to identify specific subject areas where they needed to know more in order to understand what they *didn't* yet know about the future, and for which it would be useful to have expert panels at the next workshop.

The groups reported their storylines with imagination and humour. Some of the groups came up with playful or evocative titles for their storylines, making them memorable and more resonant. (For example, a storyline that described a future in which there was no change in either authentication or regulation was titled *Head in the Sand*, while a storyline describing a future in which there was more intelligent regulation but that still retained current methods of authentication was dubbed *Half Pregnant*.)

As Roundtable members presented and discussed their storylines, it became clear that there were some differences of opinion about which uncertainties were likely to be critically important, as well as different assumptions about how ideas should best be grouped and how they related to one another (e.g., which was cause and which was effect).

Roundtable members also agreed that they needed additional information on several subjects in order to develop a fuller understanding of their likely impact on the future of payments. These included authentication, security and privacy, B2B payments, user adoption, and international developments (including methods of governance) in payments systems.

Reflections on the Workshop

At the end of the Framing Workshop, Roundtable members expressed considerable surprise at the amount of common ground they had found in the room, even among a very diverse group of stakeholders. For many this indicated an unexpected opportunity to make dramatic progress on a difficult shared problem, and they were hopeful that the workshops might provide what one member called "a trail of breadcrumbs" leading to workable solutions.

At the same time many expressed concerns about where the Roundtable process would lead and whether it would be successful. Would it be able to deal with the complexity of the issue? How would the group deal with the conflicts that would inevitably surface as they delved more deeply into details and specific approaches? Would the discussion be dominated by discussion of new technology or would it delve into the institutional and governance issues at stake? Yet throughout all these concerns there was a clear thread of common purpose and commitment to the process: a payments community had begun to develop, based on collective ownership of high-level ideas. The following are quotes from Roundtable members made at the end of the Framing Workshop.

I am feeling more hopeful and more optimistic than I was coming in here. I think we have seen everybody work together and share and become more open over the last twenty-four hours.

Collaboration is not something that we do particularly well in this industry. I think there is a real opportunity to leverage what has gone on here, to select a simple area where we can collaborate separate from or in parallel with the task force.

I think one of the positive things is that there is, at a very high level, a greater degree of commonality than one might have assumed coming into this. So I think that is extremely positive. Clearly that won't stay exactly the same once you get into the detail, but I think that is a great starting point.

When we started we were all over the place, and now we are starting to get closer not to similar approaches but to similar thoughts on what are the key issues. So I think that was a good use of our time.

We can collaborate and we can make a payment system that is a showplace for the world. The banking system here is already a showplace for security and safety, and there is an opportunity here for us working together, and getting government in, to really do something dramatic.

The biggest innovations are not in technology but around the institutions that are involved in payments. We keep talking about the actual payment flows as opposed to the institutions that are involved in the payments system. So I think we need to figure out how to address the institutional issue in the remaining sessions.

I think that there is a lot in the payments ecosystem that is very effective and still works well and can work well for us in the future. So at some point I think we need to explicitly address what is working? What can work into the future, and how do you optimize on that and build on it and enhance it?

I think it is important to recognize that to the extent that we don't work together as a redefined industry, sooner versus later it will force the need for regulation and we will end up in a reactive versus a proactive mode. I think the challenge to us is to think beyond this as being a task force and to think about how this starts to shape the redefinition of a new industry.

The next step would be to build scenarios together.

The Scenario Building Workshop

The Scenario Building Workshop took place six weeks after the Framing Workshop, in early November. The first half of this workshop was devoted to developing a better understanding of the main issues shaping the future of the Canadian payments system and, in particular, identifying those that were most important and uncertain. Expert panel presentations and Roundtable dialogues were central to this task. In the second half of this workshop, the Roundtable agreed on a framing for the scenarios, and then broke into four teams, each of which developed the timeline and narratives of one scenario. The outcome was four scenarios exploring the future of the Canadian payments system to 2020.

The workshop began with three expert panels dealing with authentication, B2B payments, and user adoption and experience – areas that Roundtable members had identified in the previous meeting as those they needed to explore further in order to fully understand the key uncertainties shaping the future. The fourth panel requested by Roundtable members – international developments in payments systems – focused on the overall dynamics of the payments system, and so was scheduled for slightly later in the workshop.

The format for these panels and subsequent discussion was the same throughout: after each set of panel presentations and a period of dialogue with the experts, the Roundtable broke into smaller groups to identify the most important or surprising insights from that panel and the most important uncertainties for the future of the Canadian payments system. After each small group reported back its conclusions, the entire Roundtable worked to compile each group's uncertainties into master lists that were then posted on the walls of the meeting room. The effect was to create an increasingly layered picture of the issues affecting the future of the payments system across an ever-expanding range of areas.

Panel 1: Authentication, Security, and Privacy

The first panel of the Scenario Building workshop was devoted to authentication, security, and privacy. The problem of online fraud was real and immediate to most Roundtable members. Merchants in the United States and Canada lost more than $4 billion to online fraud in 2008.[13] By the beginning of 2010, instances of unique malicious programs used to steal money from Internet users were running at a rate of 10,000 per year.[14] Much of this fraud was related to failures of authentication and security.

The benefits of a successful identification and verification process extend far beyond commercial transactions. For instance, a strong and secure identification process allows a patient to have a blood test in the morning, view results, and schedule a doctor visit without a phone call or e-mail. A parent can go online to view a child's school records or change his course schedule. A car owner can renew her insurance and check for outstanding fines or fees.

Greg Wolfond of Secure Key described the essential components required for someone to authenticate his or her identity. Fundamentally, he said, they boil down to:

- *what I have* (e.g., a driver's licence, credit card, or passport);
- *what I know* (e.g., a password or a piece of personal information like a first pet's name); or
- *what I am* (e.g., a fingerprint or eye scan).

In general the strongest authentication combines two or more of these methods – for example, the use of chip ("what I have") and PIN ("what I know"). But while the basics are essentially straightforward, at present authentication is fragmented, with different merchants and service providers using a range of different and often incompatible systems.

Andrew Nash, Senior Director of Identity Services at PayPal, suggested a private sector solution: an identity broker who can provide an easy-to-use interface between the consumer and myriad service providers. Such a broker would provide consumers with a single identity for accessing sites and conducting business online, removing the need to fill out forms and enter passwords while travelling around the Net.

Finally Peter Watkins, Executive Director in the Office of the British Columbia CIO, outlined several highly specific ways the government and the private sector will need to work together to achieve the next generation of public and private online services.[15]

Uncertainties: Authentication, Security, and Privacy

Based on this panel and the ensuing discussion, Roundtable members identified a number of key uncertainties related to authentication, security, privacy, and the Canadian payments system.

- **Authentication and identification**: Who will be the trust-worthy entity that runs the authentication system? What roles should the private and public sectors play? Who are the key players and how do we get them to work together? What will be the legal framework? Who pays? How will the issue of standards be dealt with? How and when will roll-out take place?
- **Privacy**: Can technology be used to protect privacy? Not adequately addressing privacy can derail identity services and digital transaction developments.
- **Role of government(s)**: Is government up for this challenge? Is government sufficiently capable, and what is the liability model? It may be that government won't get it right the first time, and if so what will be the fallout?
- **Consumer reaction**: How will consumers react? Do they want this? How will they understand the implications? Who is responsible for consumer education? How do we ensure that authentication and security are "user centric" not "enterprise centric"?

Panel 2: Business-to-Business (B2B) Payments

The Roundtable's next expert panel shifted the focus from financial services and retail to business-to-business transactions (B2B).

Vince D'Agostino and D'Arcy Delamere of JP Morgan Chase gave an overview of the global B2B marketplace, which now approaches $100 trillion in annual payments volume, of which the Canadian share in 2008 was around $2.5 trillion.

Andrew Dresner of Oliver Wyman highlighted the differences in economic models between payments made between consumers and businesses (B2C/C2B) and those made between businesses (B2B).

Finally Mike McDerment, founder and CEO of FreshBooks, offered a user's perspective on developing online payments for the small business environment. His presentation showed both the demand for online payments in the B2B space and a few of the challenges he had encountered in dealing with legacy systems.[16]

Uncertainties: B2B Payments

In their discussion and reflection, members of the Roundtable saw the question of B2B as one of the most critical areas going forward.[17] Small and medium-sized enterprises (SMEs) generate the biggest share of national revenue, and yet no one is adequately addressing SME payments. Closing this gap would be a high priority for any future system. The Roundtable identified the following uncertainties surrounding the future of B2B and the Canadian payments system:

- **Overcoming legacy systems**: What are the barriers to eliminating cheques and other older tools like international wire and the Society for Worldwide Interbank Financial Telecommunication (SWIFT)? What should be done with legacy systems and what economic model should we follow? How will that model relate to or depend on legacy systems? Are the banks prepared to replace their legacy systems?
- **Benefits to business**: What are the benefits of each system (electronic data interchange [EDI], cheque, Automated Clearing House [ACH], and electronic funds transfer [EFT]) for small, medium-sized, and large business markets? Are we serious about straight-through processing (STP) and facilitating better remittance information? What are the real issues in purchase-to-pay (e-invoicing)?
- **New standards**: What standards will be used? How will they be developed and adopted?

Panel 3: Consumer Adoption and Experience

The third expert panel of the workshop brought the perspective of users and consumers to the forefront.

Mickey McManus, President and CEO of MAYA Design, discussed how technology is evolving faster than our ability to use it, so that we need to pay more attention to making adoption simpler. He emphasized that the key to broad consumer adoption is to design around users, and provided many examples of how this has been done in practice.

Michael Adams, President of Environics, provided a perspective on social values in Canada. He identified four different broad value groups in Canada. Adams noted that each of these groups is likely to have a different mental posture towards possible changes to the Canadian payments system. The segmentation suggests that take-up of technology will not be uniform and may take a long time to reach all in the population. However, there is a sizeable part of the population prepared to experiment with new ideas.

Juliette Powell, a media entrepreneur, presented three major revolutionary trends: crowd funding, micro-transactions in social gaming, and rapidly scaling affinity networks such as Facebook. Powell suggested that the many opportunities for micro-transactions offered by these affinity networks may herald a coming revolution – imagine the impact on payments in a world where Facebook becomes the world's largest bank ("Facebank").[18]

Uncertainties: Consumer Adoption and Experience

As they reflected on the perspectives presented by this panel, Roundtable members identified the following critical uncertainties for the future of the Canadian payments system:

- **The risks and benefits of radical change of the Canadian payments system:** What are the risks of *not* keeping up with the digital economy – both structural risks and risks related to fraud? What is the power of crowd funding? What is the future of cash?
- **The appropriate level of government intervention:** Regulation of payments and privacy is uncertain. What are the needed standards and rules? What should the scope of regulation be? How will coexistence of micropayments, credits, and so forth, be managed? What will be the rules around fraud and misuse in "Facebank"?
- **Consequences for consumers:** Is user power growing? How big and significant is the digital "grey" economy? Business models will need to work across all stakeholders. How quickly are merchants/consumers going to change?

Critical Uncertainties and Focal Questions

After taking in this almost dizzying array of information and perspectives, Roundtable members faced the task of grouping, synthesizing, and refining the many lists of uncertainties they had amassed over the course of the expert panels, the previous workshop, the interview reports, and their own experience. These lists now papered nearly every vertical surface in the room, each presenting a new layer, a new wrinkle, or another perspective.

People were encouraged to walk around and take in this kaleidoscope of uncertainties. Their guiding questions were simple: On these lists, what did they believe were the most critical uncertainties that will shape the future of the Canadian payments system? And how might they map or group a list of these critical uncertainties into two or three overarching focal questions?

The resulting discussion was complex and at times challenging, as it usually is in this kind of process. Many Roundtable members had different perspectives on which uncertainties would be most critical. Some were concerned that their own issues might get pushed aside or that they might become targets for other stakeholders' resentments. (It was striking that, for a short while at this stage of the workshops, participants began moving their chairs so they were seated with others from their sector – bankers with bankers, merchants with merchants, and so on – signalling a kind of "circling of the wagons" in the face of potential challenge or disruption.)

But the sense of community Roundtable members had begun to create held firm: after working together so intensively over several days in two workshops they had built reservoirs of mutual understanding and trust. They could see the outlines of significant and exciting change beginning to take shape. And they had – and held to – the rules of dialogue.

Focal Questions

After intense discussion Roundtable members arrived at a list of what they agreed were the most critical uncertainties affecting the future of payments in Canada. With this list established, Roundtable members then organized the questions further by choosing and formulating two overarching focal questions. The final formulation of the critical uncertainties selected to frame and differentiate the scenarios was as follows:

1. **How aligned or fragmented will the payments ecosystem be** (and what will the role of government be in that ecosystem)?
2. **How fast or moderate will consumer/user adoption be?**

With these two focal questions, the Roundtable had arrived at a turning point. Now they shifted to the creative task of imagining a set of credible futures for the Canadian payments system. The rest of the Scenario Building Workshop was marked by steadily increasing energy and excitement as the Roundtable took on this task.

Creating the Scenario Set

The Canadian payments system scenario-building process employed a "deductive" approach, one that identified the most important uncertainties about the future then used these uncertainties as axes defining a grid or matrix.[19] In this case the matrix was defined by the two focal questions. These two questions formed the axes of a grid, and each quadrant represented a potential scenario (see figure 3.1).

Each Roundtable member then signed up to work on a team that would develop one of these potential scenarios, envisaging how it would play out through the year 2020.

- Team 1: Fragmented Ecosystem/Moderate rate of adoption
- Team 2: Fragmented Ecosystem/Fast adoption
- Team 3: Aligned Ecosystem/Moderate rate of adoption
- Team 4: Aligned Ecosystem/Fast adoption

The four scenario teams were diverse, each one including Roundtable members from across the different sectors. So the resulting set of four scenarios each reflected the insights of a wide

Figure 3.1: The First Definition of the Scenarios Set for the Future of the Canadian Payments System

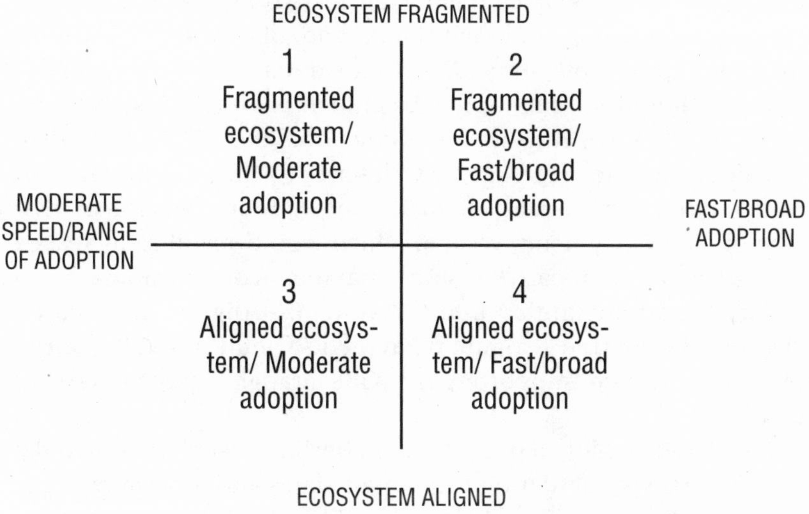

ECOSYSTEM FRAGMENTED

	1 Fragmented ecosystem/ Moderate adoption	2 Fragmented ecosystem/ Fast/broad adoption	
MODERATE SPEED/RANGE OF ADOPTION			FAST/BROAD ADOPTION
	3 Aligned ecosys- tem/ Moderate adoption	4 Aligned ecosys- tem/ Fast/broad adoption	

ECOSYSTEM ALIGNED

range of stakeholders, rather than being easily pigeonholed as the "bankers' scenario" or the "consumers' scenario."

Panel 4: International Developments in Payments

After the Roundtable members had self-selected themselves into one of the scenario teams, they reconvened for the last of the expert panels. Like the first three panels, this panel provided additional information requested by Roundtable members. However, coming as it did after the definition of the focal questions and scenario matrix, the focus was less on identifying key uncertainties and more on jumpstarting the work of the scenario teams. The developments discussed focused on Europe, Australia, and the United States.

Dave Birch, Director of Consult Hyperion, opened with a presentation on the changing landscape of retail payments in Europe, where the combination of "touch and go" contactless payments and mobile phone technology is opening up many innovative opportunities and reducing the importance of cash and paper transactions. In the B2B space there is an increasing use of electronic cheques, invoicing, and remittance and of real-time, account-to-account payments (immediate funds transfer).

Chris Hamilton, CEO of the Australian Payments Clearing Association (APCA), reviewed the development of the Australian payments system. He began by describing the traditional Australian payments system. He then reviewed the elements of a vision of a new payments system, which would result in increased competition as non-card consumer payments organizations, such as PayPal, are integrated into the system. A digital cloud-based clearing system (the "Common Payments Cloud") is at the centre of the new system, supporting the widest range of payment forms on offer.

Finally Steve Mott, a principal of BetterBuyDesign, reviewed the ongoing transformations in the United States and especially issues related to the use and regulation of credit and debit cards, and their implications for the growth of digital transactions through social networks and mobile technology.[20]

Implications for Scenarios and for Governance

After the presentations, the Roundtable teams discussed their scenarios with the expert panellists, focusing in particular on the implications of the developments the experts had highlighted for their respective scenarios. Members of all four scenario teams were especially struck by how fast things have changed in other nations, and they asked about the specifics of how different policies and regulatory frameworks had played out on the ground. Many of their questions touched on issues of governance: how do different systems get their stakeholders into some kind of alignment? What are the impacts of different regulatory frameworks when dealing with disruptive technological change? What are the costs and benefits of having to adapt to the frameworks established by other countries versus getting out in front and establishing the standard?

Building the Individual Scenarios

Following the panel the Roundtable participants worked in their scenario teams to develop their scenarios. They started by creating a brief history of the development of the Canadian payments system over the previous decade, looking at how we got where we are today, and what were the key turning points that shaped the current system. Many pointed to the successful development of Canada's Interac debit card system as a model – industry collaboration had been key to that success and likely would be essential for future payments innovation.

Next, the teams described a vision of the Canadian payments system in 2020 under their scenario: How will the payments system be structured? What will it be like to live in that world and use that payments system (for banks, for consumers, for businesses, and so on)? Finally, how will we get from today's payments system to this future? What will be the key events, changes, and milestones along the path from 2010 to 2020?

As the teams developed their scenarios they drew on one another's expertise as well as the information they had gathered over the course of the Roundtable workshops. In addition, many of the experts from the earlier panels stayed through this portion of the workshop, providing input and suggestions to the scenario teams as requested.

Before the end of the meeting each team presented an initial draft of its scenario narrative and incorporated feedback from the rest of the Roundtable and the expert panellists. Each team also chose an evocative name for its scenario – one that captured not only its impact but also its "feel." The four scenarios for exploring the future of the Canadian payments system were:

Scenario 1 (Fragmented ecosystem/moderate adoption): "Groundhog Day"
Scenario 2 (Fragmented ecosystem/rapid adoption): "Tech-tonic Shift"
Scenario 3 (Aligned ecosystem/moderate adoption): "Canada Geese"

Scenario 4 (Aligned ecosystem/rapid adoption): "Internet Inukshuk"

The logic linking the drivers, focal questions, branching points, and the four scenarios is illustrated below in figure 3.2:

Figure 3.2: Canadian Payments System Scenarios: Branching Points

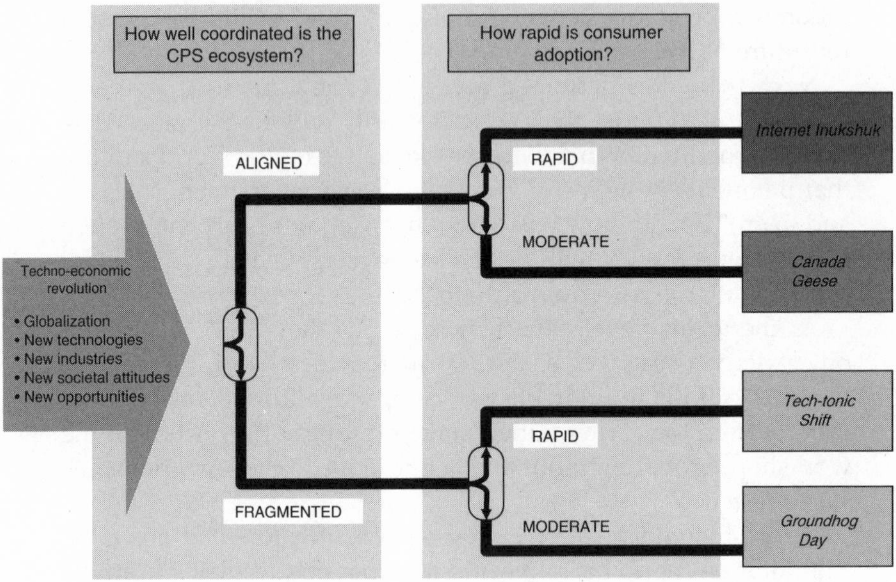

Scenario Building Workshop – Reflections

At the end of the Scenario Building Workshop, Roundtable members reflected on the workshop and the scenario building process:

> I think the possibility of collaboration is real and palpable, and I think that is much, much greater than I anticipated when I walked into the room.

The bottom line is I'm really proud to be Canadian, because I don't think there are very many places where you can get a group of stakeholders like this together and have such a collaborative discussion about the way things could evolve.

There has been amazing dialogue. People are actually talking.

We are not going fast enough. Even in the status quo scenario there are so many things that could happen that it is mind-boggling. Even the high customer adoption scenario is not really aggressive enough to deal with the kind of future we are facing.

Government can't be just a participant. It's actually going to have to lead. They are a significant issuer of cheques, we are going to have to make sure that they put their money where their mouth is and actually participate and drive some of the change.

This has been a real catalyst – an opportunity for collaboration that goes beyond these workshops and roundtables.

It was becoming clear to all participants that no matter which way forward the Canadian payments system took, greater industry collaboration – both within Canada and across borders – would be essential. And because of the pace of change (a pace that some participants thought might outstrip what was projected even in the rapid-change scenarios), collaboration must exist in order for society to respond on a timely basis to the rapidly changing environment.

For many the Roundtable process itself was becoming a model for that kind of robust collaboration – allowing people to work together even in the face of difficult challenges and differences of opinion and priorities. They were beginning to see ways that the collaboration they had begun in the Roundtable could extend far beyond its confines, catalysing changes and policies on a national or even international scale. The meeting ended on a note of optimism and anticipation – for the further development of the scenarios over the next few weeks and the prospect of sharing them with a larger group at the next meeting.

Ongoing Scenario Development between Workshops

In the weeks following the Scenario Building Workshop the draft scenarios were further refined in extensive meetings and conference calls with each scenario team. The result was the following four draft scenarios, which were presented to a larger group of stakeholders at the next workshop. Each scenario summary describes its key dimensions (how this scenario is positioned relative to the focal questions) and the rationale for the scenario's name. Originally these also included a detailed timeline of events imagining how this scenario might come to be over the next decade, but these (long and complex) timelines are not reproduced here.

Scenario 1: "Groundhog Day"

Why "Groundhog Day"? Like the movie of the same name, this scenario replays the recent past. Canada's payments system continues muddling along, and old patterns repeat themselves.

Key Dimensions
1. **Fragmented ecosystem:** In this scenario there is little change in payments system infrastructure. The major players – banks, businesses, and wireless carriers – protect their own interests, with few or no universal standards. Government lets market forces play out and intervenes only when necessary. The regulatory environment responds slowly and offers only basic protections, except when specific crises force a more significant response.
2. **Moderate consumer adoption:** Consumers and businesses are slow to use new technology. Mobile payments move slowly, and concerns about authentication, privacy, and security remain high. Small-scale innovations are launched; many ultimately fail. Without clear product winners, consumers have little incentive to embrace new technology. Many are frustrated by the limited options available, especially compared to those found in other countries. By not investing in infrastructure improvements today, Canada risks making future reforms even more disruptive and expensive.

Scenario 2: "Tech-tonic Shift"

Why "Tech-tonic Shift"? Innovative new technologies and market forces trigger a tectonic shift in the way Canadians conduct transactions, and shake their confidence in the stability of the system.

Key dimensions
1. **Fragmented ecosystem:** Major technology companies enter the payments system and become significant players. These include technology companies such as PayPal, Google, Apple, and social networking sites such as Facebook. Multi-player agreements between wireless carriers, banks, and handset manufacturers have a major impact on traditional financial institutions, which no longer dominate the payments space. Competition is fierce, with numerous alliances among players and many different interfaces and authentication systems. Government is slow to regulate until a major breach in 2015 forces its hand.
2. **Rapid consumer adoption:** Consumers and businesses embrace a wide range of new products, which they access from their e-wallets via mobile devices and online. There is a rapid proliferation of new financial services and apps. "Contactless" devices with near-field communication (NFC) ability are widely adopted by consumers and retailers. Small and medium-sized businesses are able to leverage these new payment technologies to increase their market presence, within Canada and globally.

Scenario 3: "Canada Geese"

Why "Canada Geese"? Like geese flying high in formation, the payments system players – banks, networks, third party payment service providers, merchants, industry associations, wireless carriers, governments, and others – operate within a common framework and all take turns at leading the flock.

Key dimensions
1. **Aligned ecosystem:** All payments system players are brought into the system and operate on a level playing field and within

a common framework. They agree together on standards and rules of engagement, motivated by a desire to maximize efficiency and stability. While government provides oversight at a high level, the overall system moves towards greater industry self-governance.

2. **Moderate consumer adoption:** Innovation tends to happen incrementally, because the stability and efficiency of the existing system creates less pressure to adopt newer and riskier technologies. Instead, the focus is on making the gradual, thoughtful innovations that are needed to keep the system running smoothly. Canada is moderate in adopting new approaches, taking the time to carefully evaluate potential changes and get all players on board. This more moderate pace pays off in the long run: once an idea has proven itself, the high level of collaboration allows widespread adoption.

Scenario 4: "Internet Inukshuk"

Why "Internet Inukshuk"? In a world of rapid technological change, Canadian institutions come together to lift the stones and build a great Canadian payments system for a new era. It is a guide to other countries – showing the way forward!

Key dimensions
1. **Aligned ecosystem:** There is growing awareness, in industry and more broadly, of the magnitude and speed of the changes being fuelled by cloud computing and the Internet – disrupting existing business models and ways of working, while creating huge new opportunities. Nowhere is both the threat and opportunity clearer than in Canada's payments system. Responding to this challenge, the industry comes together to create a new "Canadian Payments Council" (or CPC). The CPC facilitates the development of standards in key areas of payment, especially around privacy, security, digital ID, and authentication, and encourages competition and innovation.
2. **Rapid consumer adoption:** Canadian consumers and businesses quickly embrace a wide range of new, user-friendly, and cost-effective payment types. Keys to this rapid adoption are:

- secure authentication principles that underpin the same standards off- and online;
- the principle that Canadians "own their own data" and the accompanying leading-edge security and authentication systems that are developed;
- rigorous standards and adequate education programs.

Companies use cloud computing and collaborative networks to quickly set up payments businesses in response to consumer needs. Lessons learned in payments quickly flow to other sectors, such as health care.

The Confirmation Workshop

Sharing the Canadian Payments System Scenarios

Six weeks after the Scenario Building Workshop, the Confirmation Workshop introduced these scenarios – using the above descriptions – to a larger group of stakeholders. Those invited were senior executives from a wide range of sectors, including government; consumer groups; banking; financial services; and small and large retail, manufacturing, communications, and technology companies. They were asked to review the scenarios and offer suggestions for improvement, first by reviewing and discussing all four scenarios in mixed-sector groups and then through a second discussion with other members of their specific sectors.

The workshop began with a "Scenario Carousel," in which each scenario was presented in a separate breakout room by the Roundtable team leaders for that scenario. Participants were divided into four groups of approximately twenty-five people, with each group including a mixture of Roundtable members and new stakeholder participants from a variety of sectors. Each large group started in a different room, hearing and discussing the team leaders' descriptions of their scenario and its future timeline of events from the present until the year 2020.

In each room participants were, in a sense, given an opportunity to "live" in the world of that scenario. At the end of each thirty-minute "stop" on the carousel, the participants moved on to the next room and the next scenario, so that by the end of the two-hour carousel all four groups had seen all four scenarios.

Post-Carousel Feedback

After the carousel, the groups returned to their tables and worked in mixed-sector groups over lunch to consider how each scenario might be improved by being made more realistic and more useful. In particular, the groups were asked to consider the following questions about each scenario:

- What is implausible and why?
- What should be removed from the scenario and why?
- What is missing and should be added?

The stakeholders offered a great deal of specific feedback on the scenario content,[21] including requests for more detail about privacy, security, globalization, and B2B issues. Their comments also highlighted some important themes across the scenarios. As they looked into the future outlined by the scenarios, stakeholders quickly saw that the pace of adoption, even under the most moderate projections, would quickly overwhelm existing structures. This meant that the scenarios built around a relatively fragmented payments ecosystem (Groundhog Day and Tech-tonic Shift) were widely seen as less desirable but also more likely unless significant steps were taken. As a result the discussion turned to what kind of governance structures would be needed to align the many players, from companies to consumers, provincial governments, and international systems.

Stakeholder-Specific Feedback

The participants then divided into four stakeholder-specific clusters. While there were more than four distinct groups of stakeholders in the room, the clusters grouped people with common interests. The four clusters were: 1) Banks and other incumbents;

2) new entrants and non-traditional players; 3) large users (mostly major retailers); and 4) smaller users, including merchants and consumer groups.

In this session, the scenario team leaders went from cluster to cluster to answer questions and solicit additional feedback on their scenario. All the stakeholder clusters were asked to consider the following questions from the perspective of their individual sectors:

• What are the main strategic challenges you will face under this scenario?
• What actions will be needed to handle this scenario?
• What are the most important preparations you could undertake in the next two years?

When participants began to look at the scenarios from the perspective of their specific sectors, their responses focused on what their industries/organizations needed to do to prepare the groundwork for significant changes in the payments system. Bankers and other incumbents spoke of the urgent need to expand their services, especially in e-commerce, mobile payments, and B2B. New entrants focused on how best to build on existing investments and infrastructure, as well as connecting Canada more fully to developments in the rest of the world. Large users looked at the business case for greater alignment and cooperation. Small users focused on ensuring transparency and removing barriers to access for all.

There was also a great deal of common ground across the sector-specific clusters: all of them emphasized the need for consumer protection, well-enforced standards, and a coherent regulatory framework that would oversee coordination and cooperation. All of them also spoke of the importance of public education and engagement.

As they left the workshop, the stakeholders reflected on the process. Many appreciated the coherent introduction to possible futures for the payments system and insight into how those futures might affect them. In addition, the process had done a great deal to engage them in thinking about the role they might play in shaping those futures and had prepared them to take the conversation to their own constituencies.

Scenario Team Feedback

After the invited stakeholder participants left the workshop, the Roundtable members worked in their scenario teams to incorporate their feedback and update the scenarios. Each of the teams arrived at several adjustments to be made in their scenarios:

Scenario 1: Groundhog Day. The Groundhog Day team agreed that the stasis predicted in their scenario would likely not last for many years in today's rapidly changing landscape. Government, they said, would at some point be forced to intervene to avoid a crisis, possibly around security and authentication or instigated by foreign "500-pound gorillas." They predicted this crisis would result in further disruption, as stakeholders jockeyed for advantage and federal and provincial jurisdictions operated at cross purposes. As they saw it, a risk-averse public policy could well create a bigger risk of overreacting/over-regulating in the event of a major shock.

Scenario 2: Tech-tonic Shift. The Tech-tonic Shift team decided to focus mainly on how their scenario would impact Canadian players and their infrastructure and focus somewhat less on global players. They also reconsidered whether the system they envisaged would realistically coalesce as quickly as they had assumed, given the fragmented environment. While Canadians might recognize the need to create a consortium, as the scenario had visualized, could this realistically happen within eighteen months?

Scenario 3: Canada Geese. The Canada Geese team identified developing a common industry-driven framework as the key objective of their scenario, reasoning that if industry does not act together, government will act on its behalf. The common framework they envisaged would be backed by government and include policy advice and direction (standards), and a self-regulating, *industry-driven* organization with membership from both incumbents and new players. The team saw many benefits and opportunities arising from this framework, especially in regard to authentication, mobile standards, B2B payment options, expanded infrastructure, reduced transaction costs, and increased GDP.

Scenario 4: Internet Inukshuk. The Internet Inukshuk scenario team responded to the critique that their scenario was at times too focused on technology and not enough on the concerns of users: their approach to collaboration must address business models and "who gets what." They also decided to rename their scenario "Own the Podium" – a reference to Canada's Olympic strategy in the 2010 Winter Olympics, which had resulted in an unprecedented number of gold medals for Canadian athletes. The team felt that this new name reflected the scenario's highly proactive approach, as well as underscoring Canada's stature as a future global leader in the payments arena.

Analysis, Examples, and Metrics

Finally, the Roundtable members considered what analysis, examples, and metrics would be needed to further flesh out each of the scenarios and prepare them for distribution to a broader audience.

Conclusion: "We Have Our Scenario!"

Once these examples and metrics had been identified, the scenario development process neared its conclusion: after this meeting the scenario teams clarified their narratives, which were then written up in a more engaging style that could be used with a general audience. The final version of the scenarios as released in spring 2011 is available at: http://paymentsystemreview.ca/wp-content/themes/psr-esp-hub/documents/r01_eng.pdf. A brief summary can be found in the appendix of this book.

By the end of the Confirmation Workshop, the scenarios were both broader and deeper than when they had first been conceived, and they reflected Roundtable members' by now more nuanced understanding of the scenarios' impact on many different stakeholders. The framing of the scenarios also revealed a shift in Roundtable members' thinking about payments in Canada: rather than framing the issue in terms of financial institutions dealing with payments, they now thought in terms of a more inclusive *payments industry* involving a wide range of players, from banks to wireless carriers and technology companies to merchants to consumers.

The culmination of the scenario process also revealed the growing consensus that the future would almost certainly involve rapid, widespread technological change and that a highly aligned payments ecosystem would be the most effective way of responding to that change. In other words there was a growing consensus that a version of the "Own the Podium" scenario was both desirable and necessary.

This conviction manifested itself in a very tangible way as each team presented the near-final version of its scenario. For three of the four scenarios, members of other teams clustered loosely nearby to listen and offer feedback. Strikingly, though, when the "Own the Podium" team began its presentation, the rest of the Roundtable did not simply stand nearby – they physically moved their chairs to get closer, some of them scooting across the meeting space to get nearer to the action. The effect was electric: people physically coalesced around their preferred future, and the discussion moved quickly from how to strengthen the scenario to how to bring it about.

This kind of wholesale embrace of a specific scenario is quite unusual – it is far more common for people to use scenarios as guideposts for assessing where they are, where they would like to go, and how best to move forward. In this case, though, it quickly became clear that there was enough energy and commitment in the room to begin assembling working groups and tackling the task of designing the future and its governance processes.

As the Roundtable contemplated its final scenarios, there was rising excitement and optimism about how much had been accomplished and the potential to actually bring about significant change. Turning their attention to the final workshop, Roundtable members agreed that they wanted to "Own the Podium." The next question was how to identify the sort of institutional and governance structures that would be needed to support that framework.

chapter four

Developing a Governance Framework for the Canadian Payments System

While the Roundtable was engaged in scenario development, the Payments Task Force embarked on a parallel effort to develop a governance model for the emerging payments industry. As described below, this effort began with a traditional rather than a catalytic approach.

Challenges Facing Canadian Payments System Governance

The payments system as it existed in 2010 faced several challenging governance problems. First and most fundamental, there was *no overarching governance framework* for payments: from a legislative standpoint "payments" as a function did not exist. Various regulating bodies had oversight over different aspects of the system – the Office of the Superintendent of Financial Institutions (OFSI) regulated banks, the Bank of Canada oversaw large-value clearing and settlement, and the Financial Consumer Agency of Canada (FCAC) dealt with consumer issues in insurance and banking – but there was little or no coordination between them on payments. For the most part, regulation took an institutional rather than a functional approach: regulations applied to banks, but many payment forms and market participants fell under different provincial regulatory umbrellas or stood outside regulation altogether.[1] Regulation of clearing and settlement was similarly inconsistent: some networks (such as Interac) were scrutinized closely, while others (including MasterCard and Visa) were not. In addition, governance of some key elements of the system (for instance the clearing and settlement infrastructure operated by the Canadian Payments Association [CPA]) was dominated by banks and credit unions. This arrangement had made sense, given the systemic risk created by the delayed clearing and settlement of transactions using legacy mainframe systems. But with payments in Canada now expanding exponentially beyond the services traditionally offered by banks and credit unions (including the introduction of new technologies and even new currencies), a host of new players needed access to clearing and settlement if the overall system was to flourish.

The second major governance challenge facing the payments system was that *regulation was not keeping up with the dramatic reshaping of the industry* that was taking place. New participant types and payment forms flooded the marketplace, from PayPal and Google Pay to Bitcoin, but existing regulations did not cover them. Connected computers, combined with wireless technology and smart devices, were making it possible for non-financial companies to process payments faster and more efficiently and to collect massive amounts of data as they did so. But there was no mechanism to ensure that the resulting security and privacy concerns would be addressed. Of even greater concern was the fact that the governance framework was not robust or flexible enough to accommodate these changes: even when changes were patently required, there was no effective mechanism for making sure those changes took place, and payments users lacked an effective forum to work with payment service providers to resolve issues.

The third major challenge was the *lack of governance or a clear code of conduct for non-traditional forms of currency* such as virtual money, gift cards, or loyalty reward points, which were proliferating throughout the economy. It seemed every merchant, both online and offline, had its own program or format, most of them incompatible with the others, with no clear standards or consumer protection when it came to issues like devaluation or expiry. As these payment forms were becoming more prevalent, value and risk were accumulating outside the regulated system. It was clear that they held the potential to develop into grey market or alternative currencies that would become even more risky when they started interacting with the "mainstream" payments system.

The Payments Task Force was created in part with the mandate to bring some clarity to this dysfunctional and ineffective regulatory situation. For two years prior to the creation of the task force, merchants had been lobbying the government to do something about the escalating discount fees they paid on credit card transactions. Consumer groups were very concerned about the lack of protection and the lack of consistency and transparency in how various types of payments were treated. Small and medium-sized businesses were tired of being "nickel and dimed to death" by bank charges for payment services. Large corporations and governments could not get the information they needed to automate their processing of receivables and payables. New entrants were tentative, largely because of the uncertain regulatory environment. And users did not feel they had a meaningful voice in governing the industry. A voluntary code of conduct established to address these issues was proving inadequate.

A governance and regulatory solution was urgently needed to address these thorny issues, develop more inclusive, payments-specific legislation, and create a forum where stakeholders could work together.

Developing the Proposed Governance Framework: The Traditional Approach

The task force began its search for a reformed governance model using a traditional research and consultation approach. They started by conducting extensive research into effective governance models in other nations (including the United States, the United Kingdom, the European Union, Australia, New Zealand, Mexico, and Switzerland) and in other industries, including securities and accounting. They also solicited input from a wide range of stakeholders through online, one-on-one, and group meetings. (This process has been described in more detail in chapter 2.)

These meetings and research provided essential input for the task force to begin to tackle the governance/regulation challenges facing the payments system.[2] Following extensive consultations with stakeholders, the task force developed twelve principles representing the values they believed should be reflected in the payments system.

The first six principles relate to the *values and needs* of those using the payments system. They affect the way the payments system operates.

1. **Competition and innovation:** The payments industry should be open and competitive; participants should have the ability to innovate.
2. **User access and efficiency:** All consumers, including merchants, businesses, and governments, should have access to effective, affordable payment options.
3. **Transparency and choice:** Rules, responsibilities, risks, and costs should be clear. Participants should have necessary information and tools. Payers and payees should be able to choose among a variety of payment forms without undue penalties.
4. **Fairness and accountability:** Costs should accrue to market participants who receive the associated benefits, unless another party chooses to bear those costs. All sides should understand the associated risks.
5. **Security:** All vital technologies and processes should be secure and reliable. Payers and payees should have confidence in the payments system.
6. **Privacy:** Payers should own their personal (or organizational) information, and be able to determine how it is used. Payers should have to disclose only the information necessary for a given payment.

The next six principles apply to the *oversight and administration* of the payments system, a task shared by industry and government. These principles affect the way rules and standards are set and followed in the industry.

7. **Consistent standards:** Rules for domestic payments should be consistent to ensure efficiency. Domestic standards should facilitate global interoperability.
8. **Minimal regulation:** Regulation should occur only when the open market and industry standards fail to deliver on market-related principles.
9. **Neutrality by function:** Standards and rules should be based on the activity performed not the institution performing the activity. Rules should apply consistently across function.
10. **Proportionality:** Protection should take into account the risk involved (transaction type and dollar value).
11. **Independent and inclusive:** Governance of the payments system should not be controlled by a minority of stakeholders.
12. **Framework adaptability:** Industry governance should be robust, yet flexible enough to remain relevant over time.

With this foundation, the task force embarked on a process to create a new governance framework employing a methodology called Strategic Choice Structuring™ (see figure 4.1).[3]

In contrast to traditional "boil the ocean" research strategies, Strategic Choice Structuring™ is a more disciplined way of developing, analysing, testing, and choosing strategic directions. By focusing on the barriers facing different potential choices it allows decision makers to target their analysis to the most viable solutions. It is one of the most effective tools for developing deliberate strategy, with a proven track record on a wide range of issues. But for all its strengths, this approach proved inadequate to address the kind of wicked problem represented by the Canadian payments industry.

The Payments Task Force worked through the Strategic Choice Structuring process in a series of meetings conducted in parallel to the Payments Roundtable. They developed and reverse-engineered several options for governance and regulation of the industry – options that spanned the continuum from no regulation, to self-regulation, to government-led regulation. Each represented a different way of resolving the differences among merchants, acquirers, networks, issuers, and consumers.

Figure 4.1: The Strategic Choice Structuring Process

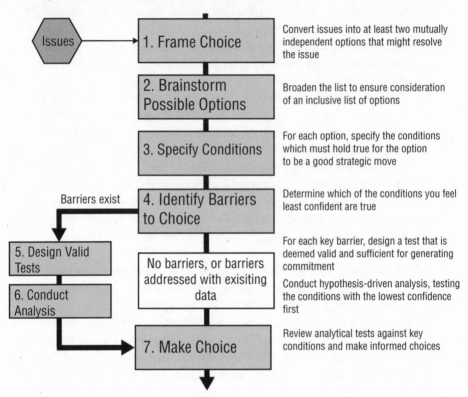

As the options developed, each one was tested against the specific regulatory issues surrounding credit/debit cards. This was an area that was timely and urgent, and also one that involved nearly every aspect of the payments industry – including banks, merchants, networks, merchant acquirers and processors, wireless carriers, and consumers.

None of the governance options identified by this method helped to resolve the issues.

For instance, improving and strengthening the code of conduct would address some of the challenges but leave unaffected many players who stand outside the code's purview. Similarly, capping the credit card fees paid by merchants (as had been done in Australia) would drive the merchant acquirers to incorporate elsewhere to avoid regulation.[4] The task force went through the process several times, engineering and testing a series of solutions, and each time found themselves squeezing a balloon – addressing part of an issue only to see it bulge out in another area. The Strategic Choice Structuring process was unparalleled at developing strategy when the likely menu of outcomes is known, but – as was becoming clear through the Roundtable discussions – the future of the payments system was all about the unknowns. This dramatically changing landscape demanded a radically different approach to solving the governance question.

Developing the Proposed Governance Framework: The Roundtable Approach

As their frustration mounted, Payments Task Force members were also taking part in the Payments Roundtable – an experience that ultimately transformed their approach to the governance challenge. Task force members found that the Roundtable discussions opened up broader thinking about what components are essential for effectively governing the payments system of the future. The open, dialogue-based process was making tremendous progress in clarifying the key drivers of the future of payments, developing a vision of a desired future (the "Own the Podium" scenario), and creating a coalition willing and able to implement the desired future.

So the task force began the Strategic Choice Structuring process over again, this time using the broader framework developed in the Roundtable process to help draft a vision of what the payments governance structure should be. To develop new options they first asked themselves what essential components must be present to effectively govern the payments system of the future. The resulting analysis had five essential components (laid out in figure 4.2). The elements reflected what the task force had learned from its work to date and combined that with new ideas resulting from their participation in the Payments Roundtable.[5]

Figure 4.2: Essential Elements of a Viable Governance Structure

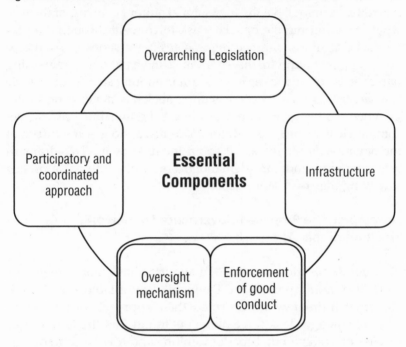

Reproduced with the permission of the Department of Finance, 2015: http://payment systemreview.ca/wp-content/themes/psr-esp-hub/documents/rf_eng.pdf

First, the governance framework would require *overarching legislation* establishing payments as a tangible, specific industry made up of a range of players involved in the transfer of value. This high-level legislation would be based on principles rather than on regulating specific players or industries, and it would be "light," allowing players to act within it rather than being restrained by it. Ideally, this legislation would remain relevant over time, despite the ongoing rapid changes in the payments industry.

The success of collaboration and dialogue in the Roundtable process made it clear that the framework should incorporate a *participatory and coordinated approach*. The governance structure would need broad industry participation in the development and implementation of the strategy. This is especially important in the setting and enforcement of standards and codes of conduct.

The governance structure would also need an accessible and efficient *infrastructure*. This infrastructure would need to be low-cost, well-functioning, and open to facilitate the entry of new players and the transition to digital payments. The infrastructure should be enhanced to offer online features, including greater data transfer, faster processing, and digital identification and authentication.

The system would need an *oversight mechanism* to identify emerging trends and issues; monitor the security, ease of access, and cost-effectiveness of payments; and provide oversight during transition periods. This entity could identify risks and opportunities and assess the effectiveness of the Canadian payments system, working with industry and government and ultimately making recommendations for improvements. And finally there needed to be a mechanism for *enforcement of good conduct*. If industry failed to uphold the principles espoused in the payments legislation, steps should be taken to ensure compliance and provide recourse if codes of conduct were not being followed or standards were not being met. Given the limits imposed by the Canadian constitution, a Payments Industry Association was the most expeditious approach.

These five essential components became the stepping stones that helped the task force create a truly viable regulatory and governance structure. Ultimately, the Proposed Governance Framework had the following four essential features (see figure 4.3):

1. Payments Legislation. Where previously payments had been governed by a patchwork of legislation, regulations, and bylaws, the new governance framework would introduce comprehensive payments-specific legislation. This legislation would define and validate the importance of payments as an industry.
2. Industry Self-Governing Organization (SGO). At the heart of the governance framework lay the realization that arose out of the Roundtable process: most problems in the payments system could be addressed only by participants – both suppliers and users – working together. For this to happen, players would need a collaborative forum, as well as provision for collective action to resolve divisive issues. To this end, the governance framework encouraged the creation of an SGO to include all payment players – users and suppliers, incumbents

Figure 4.3: Proposed Governance Framework: Canadian Payments Ecosystem

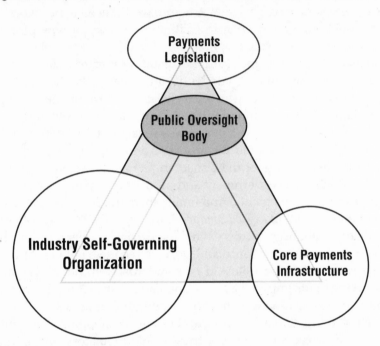

Reproduced with the permission of the Department of Finance, 2015: http://payment-systemreview.ca/wp-content/themes/psr-esp-hub/documents/rf_eng.pdf

and new entrants – who would work to develop and enforce codes of conduct and manage the adoption and integration of new technologies.

3. Basic Payments Infrastructure. Payments infrastructure should be trustworthy, efficient, low-cost, and open to all players. Canada's existing infrastructure needed to be upgraded to handle digital payments, including online features that would allow greater data transfer and faster funds transfer. To support the digital economy government needed to establish a digital identification and authentication regime.

4. Payments Oversight Body (POB). The creation of new legislation and the formation of an SGO would require oversight and

guidance, as would Canada's transition to a digital payments system, a necessary step in making Canada a global payments leader by 2020. To this end, a temporary, independent POB would be formed to monitor evolutions in payments while providing oversight during transition periods. It would identify risks and opportunities, working with industry and government to refine and improve the system. If any participant proved unable to adhere to the principles set out in the payments legislation or if codes of conduct were not observed, government regulations would ensure compliance and provide recourse.

This model reflected the developing consensus among the Roundtable members that any effective governance structure for the payments industry would have to involve all the key stakeholders. As one participant put it at the February 2011 meeting, "We need a collaborative effort for the future. I believe it's essential that we take responsibility for the payment industry ... to help the industry to regulate and be responsible for itself, instead of being regulated the old way."

As the Roundtable unfolded, Payments Task Force members recognized that it was already beginning to function as an industry self-governing organization. At Roundtable meetings, users and suppliers were working together and discussing ways to resolve their differences. These working relationships even extended to the vexing test case of credit/debit cards: during breaks and meals many key players around that issue – including bankers, networks (Visa and MasterCard), merchant acquirers, retailers, and SMEs – began discussing the credit/debit issue and the concessions each was prepared to make.

At the same time the task force was beginning to function as the temporary payments oversight body. Task force members volunteered to chair and provide resources for industry working and advisory groups to develop initiatives to reduce Canada's reliance on cheques, create a mobile ecosystem, build a digital identity and authentication regime, formalize the self-governing organization, and upgrade payments infrastructure. In effect, the Proposed

Governance Framework institutionalized the developments emerging from the Payments Roundtable process.

Final Workshop

Testing the Proposed Governance Framework

In February 2011 the Payments Roundtable met for a final workshop, in which they used the scenarios to test and further develop the Proposed Governance Framework. Roundtable participants were especially eager to begin this phase of the work and launch their desired scenario on the road to real-world implementation. They asked about the future after the conclusion of the Roundtable process: How would they maintain their momentum and how could they use that momentum to effectively catalyse broad-based change in their industry? For many the scenario process had been especially illuminating in terms of projecting a future that was both possible and desirable. They agreed that the Canadian payments system was not likely to find itself in either of the low-adoption scenarios: rapid and widespread adoption of new technology was clearly the way of the future. And as the Roundtable considered the two high-adoption scenarios, they arrived at a strong preference for the aligned ecosystem scenario, "Own the Podium," over the fragmented ecosystem represented in "Techtonic Shift." Finding the right governance system would be the key to determining which way the future would unfold.

Participants' comments at the beginning of the workshop reflect their understanding of the importance of governance and their eagerness to help shape a workable framework.

> I think one of the greatest uncertainties facing the Canadian payments system is what, exactly, will happen from a regulatory and governance perspective.

> What's exciting ... is that we now actually get to chew on the strategy and governance framework ... I'm excited about that.

I am very much looking forward to moving forward from the strategic framework that we've developed to a road map for putting [it] in place, with input from all the stakeholders.

It's good to see that we've identified a lot of the friction points [through] the scenario process. Now we need to turn that into an effective road-map planning process so we can move this at the pace it needs to go.

How will we continue to act collectively for the betterment of the Canadian payments system when we don't have the catalyst of the task force report or the meetings? My big question is how much momentum will we walk out with tomorrow?

I want to point out the momentum that I think we've already created. If I look at developments, news articles, and interaction between different companies – we are definitely helping to build the momentum and acting as a catalyst. I am looking forward to creating a powerful roadmap.

I hope and believe that in 2020 when we look back, we'll say we did something substantial and we have one of the best payment systems there is.

To all in the room, it was now clear that there was a "payments industry" that was distinct from the financial industry. One participant's opening statement captured the prevailing sentiment: "I think many have been surprised that we have been able to meet and collaborate across the whole payments industry. It's clear that everybody wants a self-determined solution, and I think we have a great opportunity to do that. I'm confident that something very concrete will come out of this."

Pat Meredith, who chaired the task force, opened the discussion by describing the Proposed Governance Framework in some detail. Roundtable participants then tested this framework against each of the scenarios to better understand how well it might work under each possible future. Working in scenario teams, participants considered which elements of the proposed framework would be especially easy or difficult to implement under their

Table 4.1 Scenario-specific Responses to the Proposed Governance Framework

	Groundhog Day	Tech-tonic Shift	Canada Geese	Own the Podium
Elements that will be easy to implement	1. Light regulation 2. Safety & soundness	Light regulation	SGO (that's what the Canada Geese scenario is all about!)	1. Participation and cooperation in Canada 2. Building "coalition of the willing" (COTW) 3. Working groups: especially digital ID 4. Industry work on mobile payments
Elements that will be difficult to implement	1. Consistency of standards 2. Fairness & accountability 3. Neutrality of function 4. Self-regulation 5. Innovation & competition	1. Need for industry definition 2. Establishing SGO 3. Evolving the huge mountain of existing legislation 4. Creating membership "tiers" – criteria? 5. Facilitating transition of existing regulation, legislation, codes, policies, and procedures 6. Enforcing compliance – who has authority, especially when international entities are involved? 7. Hierarchy & definition of members; some players highly regulated; others not 8. Not level playing field for members	1. Infrastructure, setting up clusters and working groups 2. What's in it for the proprietary networks?	1. Getting legislative changes made 2. Working with the "unwilling": they won't quit and drop out, they will quit and stay! 3. Managing self-interest in the coalition 4. Defining and finding funding for the infrastructure(s) and economic model(s) for change 5. Achieving a level playing field – especially "unleashing" the banks. Lots of people won't want to unleash banks.

Table 4.1 Scenario-specific Responses to the Proposed Governance Framework (cont.)

	Groundhog Day	Tech-tonic Shift	Canada Geese	Own the Podium
Obstacles to implementing the framework	1. Many conflicting priorities, and limited resources 2. Implementing "light" regulations in a way that is seen as legitimate 3. With many different networks, can't get economies of scale	1. Jurisdictional definition of "payments industry" 2. Cross-border issues and interoperability	1. Ownership & governance same SGO & infrastructure? 2. Dealing with/transitioning from existing institutions, structures, regulations 3. Need for strong business-case rationale for infrastructure changes – how do stakeholders and participants justify the investment?	1. Maintaining the COTW with only light legislation 2. Defining responsibilities of government & FIs for managing risks of new entrants 3. Willingness of international big players to play by Canadian rules

Actions that might help address obstacles	1. Focus on:
	  a. Governance
	  b. Digital ID & authentication
	  c. How to remove cheques
	  d. Need to address network imbalances (e.g., fees for debit/ versus credit)
	2. Government must establish governance structure for SGO & legislation
		1. Financial literacy
		2. Recognition of "approved" players
			1. Use government pressure to get system set up
			2. Establish a "no opting out" regulatory framework (if you play, you must be part of it)
			3. Build on momentum from Roundtable
				1. Analyse weaknesses in CPA infrastructure – what is needed to put in place desired future?
				2. Adopt guiding principles (e.g., regulate by function, protect Canadians' deposits). How will the older players (like PayPal) and the new ones (like Google and Facebook) be regulated?

scenario. What would be the major obstacles to implementing the framework, and how might those obstacles be overcome?

The Proposed Governance Framework was effective in each of the potential futures (see the summary in table 4.1). Governance reform was important in all the scenarios, especially for the two high-adoption scenario teams, both of which expressed the urgency of moving forward with a governance framework that captured all participants in the rapidly changing payments environment. All of the groups agreed on the importance of light regulation of the entire industry, as well as the need for a self-governing organization that could bring all the players – users and suppliers, incumbents and new entrants – to the table.

Designing the Self-Governing Organization

Pat Meredith then opened the discussion of what would be involved in establishing the self-governing organization (SGO). This organization would be a bottom-up effort by the payments industry, rather than a top-down government initiative. The design would build on the catalytic approach established by the Payments Roundtable and ensure the full participation of all stakeholders, including users and suppliers, incumbents and new entrants. Roundtable member Barbara Stymiest, a senior executive at Canada's largest bank, agreed to lead a working group to design and put in place the foundation for an SGO.

Participants then divided into smaller groups, each made up of a cross-section of stakeholders and members from each scenario team. These groups worked together to draft potential models for the SGO, considering its role, mandate, and membership; how it should be organized and funded; and its relationship to government.

The Roundtable then compared the groups' conclusions and agreed on a basic design and structure for the SGO:

The SGO's *role and mandate* would be to:

• ensure full collaboration, involving all stakeholders;
• address both global and local matters that affect the success of the Canadian payments system;

- set and enforce standards/codes of conduct, and where necessary impose sanctions;
- track emerging trends/innovations;
- optimize a payments system for the Canadian economy and advise government as appropriate;
- emphasize and ensure full and open competition in payments.

Membership in the SGO would be mandatory: anyone wishing to provide payments services in Canada would be required to be a member in good standing.

The SGO would be organized around a *board and assembly*. The SGO assembly would consist of forty to sixty members elected initially from eight categories: Financial Services incumbents; Networks (including credit card companies, Interac, and the CPA); Retail/Service entities; Technology Providers; Wireless Carriers; Alternative Payment Networks; Acquirers and Processers; and Consumers. Additional categories could be added as the industry continued to develop. The board of directors, elected by the assembly, would be composed of sixteen directors: six permanent members (drawn from FIs and Networks), six rotating members drawn from the other categories represented in the assembly, and four independent members.

Roundtable members also proposed the creation of *standing committees* with representation from all stakeholder groups. These committees would oversee standards and code of conduct; audit and compliance; risk, fraud, and identity; emerging payments (including R&D, trends, new ideas); and government and international relations. In addition, ad hoc working groups would deal with other issues (such as implementation of new payment mechanisms) as they emerged. These ad hoc groups would have limited mandates, scope, and duration, and would be reviewed annually by the board. In general these standing committees would include a range of stakeholders at all levels; they would need to rely on public consultation as much as possible, and their initiatives should include a significant public education focus. All standing committee recommendations would need to be approved by the board.

The Roundtable envisaged that the SGO would employ between twelve and twenty people and have a budget of about $5 million, to be *funded* by an annual membership fee.

The Roundtable also developed suggestions as to how the SGO might relate to government, as well as a detailed agenda and timeline to launch the new organization.

The SGO working group started its work with this input and a large number of volunteers from the Roundtable. Three additional advisory groups were also formed: Governance, Consumer, and Regulatory. The contributions to the process of all these groups are discussed in chapter 5.[6] At the conclusion of the workshop, the chair summarized the task force's plans for outreach. These included media and social media outreach efforts and a brief video for the public describing the evolution of payments.

In the months that followed, the SGO Working Group and Payments Task Force members further consulted with governance, regulatory, and consumer experts. In June, the task force made the Proposed Governance Framework publicly available for review and public comment in a discussion paper (*The Way We Pay*) on its website. They incorporated feedback from the Roundtable and comments made on the website and fleshed out the model with the SGO Working Group and the Governance, Consumer, and Regulatory Advisory Groups.[7] At the end of December the task force formally recommended the Governance Framework to the Finance Minister and provided extensive policy papers explaining and supporting its recommendations.

Closing Comments from Members about the Roundtable: "The End of the Beginning"

This workshop marked the end of the formal Roundtable process. As they prepared to move on to working groups and implementation, participants reflected on what one called "the end of the beginning" and what they were bringing away from the experience.

Participants especially appreciated the collaborative and inclusive effort and the trust that had developed among a diverse group with many competing interests. They recognized the power of bringing together all these major stakeholders to engage in bottom-up reform. This had built a sense of ownership and investment in the future.

The scenario process had also given participants an acute awareness of the kind of future they *didn't* want, and this reinforced their eagerness to establish the SGO. As one participant said, "We need a collaborative effort for the future. I believe it's essential that we take responsibility for the payment industry. We have to create that new SGO to help the payments industry to regulate and be responsible for itself, instead of being regulated the old way." Selected quotes from Roundtable members are shown below.

> This used to be an exclusive club. I think this process has demonstrated that it ought to be and has become an inclusive club. There has been a lot of dialogue and trust developed, and the collaboration is a good working model. Right now, we're at the end of the beginning. I encourage everybody to build on what we've established here.

> I'm very encouraged that we in this room feel like we own this as opposed to feeling like it's something that's being done to us. That's not just semantics; it's truly a difference in outlook and level of engagement.

> I fully concur that we've developed a high level of trust and respect for each other. We haven't held anything back, we've told you all we know. We've given you our entire perspective on things, and we want to work with you to get to a common goal – and we really believe we can.

Participants also appreciated a process they described as "consultative, interactive, and adaptive" – one that made the best use of the collective knowledge of all participants. Users were especially vocal in this regard, feeling that they had often been excluded from decision making in the past. Brien Gray, the Executive Vice-president of the Canadian Federation of Independent Business, said that in his thirty years of working with the government, "this was the *first time* that I felt included in the process. I have no intention of going back to the old approach."

> I want to thank you as a retailer and on behalf of my fellow merchants
> – looking at these different scenarios and outcomes it's clear that you've
> really listened to and taken in our concerns.

> The opportunity to move the payments industry to a cohesive, dialogu-
> ing, effective format is monumental. And the ability to eliminate some
> of the individual perspectives and leave them at the door is ground-
> breaking. I've been in multiple markets; I've never seen anything like
> it. And once this SGO is ultimately developed, to include the ability to
> have global interoperability, innovation, competition, and cooperation
> – that's a huge challenge.

Participants also noted that the process had helped to forge a
shared lexicon and common framework for discussing issues. The
idea that they were all part of a *payments industry* was especially
powerful (a "huge deal," one participant said, and one that "will
make a tremendous difference in how we think, how we work, and
how we interact as an industry"). Dialogue was especially important in building bridges across differences. One self-described "old
professor" put it this way: "At the beginning of the dialogue I said
to myself, 'Will these people be able to shed their affiliations and
dialogue rather than debate?' My expectation was that I was going
to give you a C on that. But at the end I think you've come in at an
A-minus!"

> At the beginning it seemed quite radical that we were talking about
> the payments industry rather than the financial industry. And that has
> become an unconscious part of our dialogue, though it may have been
> forced at the beginning.

> We did not have a common lexicon when we walked in here at the end
> of last year. We didn't really understand or agree about what the op-
> tions were – but when we sat down we saw that there were a lot more
> commonalities in our thoughts and purposes than differences. It's go-
> ing to be exciting to grab that collective thinking and turn it into collec-
> tive will and keep going over the next few months and years.

Many others were also struck by how far the group had come in just a few short months, and they drew a sharp contrast between their current enthusiasm and the doubt and scepticism that had characterized the earliest phases of the process. As one participant put it, "If everyone had had to rate our chances of success [at the beginning] there would have been a lot of Ds and Fs. You had a huge mountain to climb and you've done so exceedingly successfully." They wanted to maintain this momentum and act – not let the energy drain away. Several participants noted the need to "score some wins" in the near future to keep the momentum going and bring more people on board with the effort. "I worry when I hear it will be three to four years before we can get this completely done," said one. "I think there is traction now, and I think there's a will now, but I worry that that could wane if we don't start getting value for the effort. I'm in to help deliver on that, but we've got to push ourselves."

As they moved forward to drafting initiatives, participants recognized the need to be pragmatic and proactive going forward: for all the talk about a "higher purpose," one participant said, "we need to make sure we don't neglect the lower purpose" of making the system simpler, faster, and cheaper. This was seen as the only way to continue to broaden engagement around the effort and bring the sceptics along.

Overall, the Roundtable participants saw the process as a model for future task forces and royal commissions, as well as holding the potential to create a payments system that would be the envy of the world. "We started this whole process by saying this is uniquely doable in Canada," said one. "It makes me proud of what we can accomplish here."

I think we all have a sense this is an opportunity we have to seize and not let go. I've lived the last three years through a start-up, and we all know that's all about perseverance – we'll just keep pushing through it, whatever is needed.

My observation from working both north and south of the border is that today politicians and lawyers are designing the payment systems in North America. And they are absolutely the worst ones to be doing it – the outcomes are bad for everybody. If we don't get this right, we won't reclaim this ground where collaboration between merchants, between acquirers, between banks and everyone else can find fruitful solutions. If we let lawyers and politicians do it, it just becomes winners and losers. And the consequences of that are not good for the public. You don't get an efficient or good payment system. I started this session by saying I thought what you were doing was quite radical. I still think it is. And I only make that comment because it is so important for this to succeed. If it doesn't, I'm afraid of where we're going.

I think back to September when this started. There was a fair bit of scepticism and cynicism in the room. And the change is incredible to hear. I think you've done an incredible job with your passion and your vision and your commitment. It has brought everybody forward to the place where you were. I think the whole room has now embraced that. That is a tremendous feat; I can't believe there's been any other task force in the history of Canada that's been able to do that … You've started an important journey, and it will take some time. I think the comment was right: we have to stay committed; we need some early wins. The next steps are key to how we succeed. We need to all continue to be engaged, be part of this process, and to continue dialoguing with all the key stakeholders.

As the Roundtable prepared to adjourn, the newly appointed leader of the work on the SGO and the chair of the task force concluded the meeting with their own remarks:

SGO LEADER: I believe we're on a very good path. This collaboration between the task force and the industry is extremely positive. It needs to continue for us to be successful, both in the short-term deliverable, and in the long-term. We have a lot of work to do to work in parallel with the direction that the task force is heading, but I think it's the right thing to do. The outcomes can be game-changing for us. I look forward to the successful conclusion of the task force and the launch of the enduring body of the SGO.

TASK FORCE CHAIR: This is the end of the scenarios process, but it is the beginning for the Canadian payments industry, which has the potential to be one of the leading payments industries in the world. You can't predict the future, but you can create the future. Scenarios are in part an exercise in thinking deeply about the future, so that you can actually begin to plan steps that allow you to create the future. So I really am looking forward to working with all of you as the SGO takes on more and more of the responsibilities of creating that future, and creating a payments industry that we – and all Canadians – can all be proud of.

The Roundtable emerged from the last scenarios workshop with a strong sense of ownership, energy, and commitment to achieve the positive vision of the Canadian payment system they had created together. They were the payments industry, and they were prepared to roll up their sleeves and begin working on the initiatives necessary to make their vision a reality. Chapter 5 describes the tremendous progress they made over the next eight months.

chapter five

Co-creating a Desired Future

The "coalition of the willing" that emerged from the Payments Roundtable went forward deeply committed to helping Canada become a world leader in payments.[1] Within weeks of the last Roundtable session in February 2011 they had begun meeting in working groups to draft initiatives to transition Canada from paper-based to digital payments. This is the fourth step in the catalytic governance model.

The working groups were devoted to building a digital identification and authentication regime, implementing electronic invoicing and payments for business and government, creating a public-private mobile ecosystem, upgrading the payments infrastructure, and designing a self-governing organization (SGO) for the payments industry. In addition, three advisory groups – governance, regulatory, and consumer – were organized to help the SGO Working Group and the task force refine the Proposed Governance Framework presented in chapter 4. All this work was supported by resources from the Payments Task Force.

Many participants expressed considerable excitement about the prospect of working together to help Canada transition from a paper-based to a digital payments system – a future they could envisage clearly as a result of the scenario development process. (A précis of "Own the Podium" appears in box 5.1; the complete scenario can be found at: http://paymentsystemreview.ca/wp-content/themes/psr-esp-hub/documents/r01_eng.pdf.) The task force supported this energy and enthusiasm by enabling working and advisory groups that would begin developing and implementing concrete strategies. In effect, the task force played a catalytic role.

Box 5.1: "Own the Podium" Scenario Summary

OWN THE PODIUM

Aligned ecosystem and rapid consumer adoption

There is growing awareness of the magnitude and speed of changes being fuelled by the convergence of computing and connectivity into the smart phone, disrupting existing business models and ways of working while creating huge new opportunities. Nowhere are both the threat and the opportunity clearer than in Canada's payments system. Responding to this challenge, industry comes together to facilitate the rapid development of a set of standards in key areas of payment – especially privacy, security, digital ID and authentication, and mobile payments – that will encourage competition and innovation and enable Canada to lead developments elsewhere in the world. This effort is reminiscent of the "Own the Podium" campaign at the 2010 Olympics, when Canada moved away from traditional approaches to win the most gold medals ever for a Winter Olympics host country.

Canada sees remarkable shifts to new ways of processing payments and other transactions. The principle that Canadians "own their own data" and the accompanying robust digital identification and authentication systems that are developed are crucial in encouraging rapid consumer adoption and enabling Canada to capitalize on the massive changes under way. Companies use cloud computing and collaborative networks to set up payments businesses quickly in response to consumer needs. Lessons learned in payments quickly flow to other sectors, such as health. In financial institutions and other industries, there is much disruption and considerable job loss but also the creation of new industries and new jobs. By 2020 Canada is a global leader in this new online world, and is exporting its expertise and systems to the global community.

Emergent Strategy and Action Learning

Strategy development is especially challenging in the face of un-predictability and flux, when often we understand why things happen only in retrospect. In those circumstances, management experts have suggested, "Instead of attempting to impose a course of action, leaders must patiently allow the path forward to reveal itself."[2] That is, allowing actions to converge over time into some sort of consistency or pattern – *emergent strategy* – is the best way (if not the only way) to develop strategy in complex, rapidly chang-ing systems. This approach assumes that those responsible for de-veloping the strategy are also engaged in executing it, constantly testing and reassessing strategy as it unfolds.

We adopted an emergent approach to strategy to address the issue of transitioning to digital payments and to develop the Pro-posed Governance Framework when more traditional approaches failed. In order to enable the kind of creative testing and assess-ment needed, the Payments Task Force encouraged stakeholder working groups to determine a way forward through a process of "action learning."

Action learning is a method for enabling individual, organiza-tional, and strategic development in which people work in small groups to create options, take action, and learn from the results. Action learning has the following four elements:

1. Each person joins in and takes part voluntarily.
2. Each participant must own a managerial or organizational problem on which they want to act.
3. Sets or groups of action learners meet to help each other think through the issues and create options.
4. Participants take action and learn from the effects of that action.

Initially developed by Reginald Revans in the 1940s, action learning has been applied to a wide range of issues in a wide vari-ety of circumstances.[3] In some ways it is similar to "action re-search," which was developed by Kurt Lewin at about the same time and has also been widely applied.[4] Both approaches share

Revans's conviction that "there is no learning without action and no (sober and deliberate) action without learning." Especially relevant in the case of the task force was Revans's proposition that for organizations (or individuals or industries) to survive and thrive, their rate of learning must be at least equal to the rate of change in their external environment.

Transitioning to Digital Payments

The Payments Roundtable participants knew where Canada had to go – from paper payments to digital payments – and most were prepared to help figure out how to get there. In their discussions they identified five key areas of focus for the transition to digital payments and proposed creating stakeholder working groups for each. The five key areas were:

1. Electronic Invoicing and Payments (initially called "Reducing Cheques");
2. Mobile Payments;
3. Digital Identification and Authentication;
4. Self-Governing Organization (Payments Industry Association); and
5. Payment Processing, Clearing, and Settlement Infrastructure. The first three groups focused on transitioning to digital payments, and groups four and five focused on questions of governance.

Almost every participant in the Payments Roundtable volunteered to join at least one of these working groups; in addition, nearly 200 other stakeholders signed on to take part in the working groups and related subcommittees. The groups extended and strengthened the sense of a more inclusive "payments industry" that had been established during the Payments Roundtable as well as building momentum around the effort to create a new payments ecosystem. The working groups were broadly tasked with developing emergent strategies to transition the Canadian payments ecosystem to online digital payments. Over the next nine months, the working groups addressed the first four areas: participants got together, decided what they wanted to accomplish, and developed initiatives to achieve those goals. The fifth working group (payment processing, clearing, and settlement) was slower to come together, largely because the managers of the current infrastructure – most of whom had not participated in the Payments Roundtable – were reluctant to engage with the broader payments community and each other.

Task force members took on the role of chairing the groups and capturing the emerging strategy,[5] as well as supplying independent consultants to manage administration and conduct research. Each of the working groups produced detailed roadmaps to manage the transition from the old world to the new one, ready to hand them over to the SGO whenever it was created. All of the work described in the following pages was ultimately captured by the task force in the discussion paper *Going Digital*[6] and in the policy papers[7] supporting the recommendations on governance and infrastructure.

Working Group 1: Electronic Invoicing and Payments (EIP)

The Electronic Invoicing and Payments (EIP) Working Group was formed to accelerate the adoption of B2B electronic payments. Although Canada was a leader in digital retail point-of-sale (POS) payments, it trailed behind most developed countries, including the United States, in B2B electronic payments. Only 39 per cent of business and government payments in Canada were made electronically, compared with the leaders, Germany and the Nordic countries, which had achieved upwards of 95 per cent B2B electronic payment rates. Canada's ongoing reliance on paper cheques is placing a drag on the economy compared to these other, more forward-looking nations.

Based upon its research into the experiences of other countries in converting to digital payments – including the Nordic Countries, the United Kingdom, and the United States – the EIP working Group set itself the goal of eliminating 80 per cent of the cheques in Canada by 2020. The task was not simple. Changing the payments systems used by Canadian businesses and governments would require ongoing coordination and investment. That said, the right combination of government leadership and industry participation would yield annual savings of between $7 billion and $8 billion.[8] Savings for large enterprises from transitioning to digital payments and automating the end-to-end accounts receivable and payable processing were estimated at $5 billion per year, with small and medium-sized organizations and financial institutions capturing $700 million and $600 million, respectively. Even more important than the massive savings, a modern payments system using the latest technology would support the development of products and services leading to far greater choice, efficiency, and convenience for consumers, businesses, governments, and organizations, as well as a safer and more secure system.

At more than 100 members, the EIP Working Group was the largest and most diverse collaboration, comprising federal and provincial governments, large corporations, small and medium-sized enterprises, banks, insurance companies and credit unions, accountants, software vendors, and network providers. With a mandate to recommend efficient and secure end-to-end electronic payment alternatives for businesses and governments, the working group was structured around a single steering committee and several subcommittees. (Subcommittees included large corporate and governments, small and medium-sized businesses, government and insurance company payments to individuals, standards and technology roadmap, and integration and economics.) Initially, two-thirds of the working group members were users and one-third suppliers. However, as suppliers began to recognize the business opportunities they were missing, more asked to join the working group and its subcommittees.

For eight months, the EIP Working Group sought ways of bringing Canada into the digital age. Its work led to eight initiatives. The first three fell under the domain of governments, both federal and provincial:

1. Support the phase-out of consumer cheques issued and received by government;

2. Drive government adoption of e-invoicing and payments; and
3. Launch a campaign to communicate vision for the digital economy.

The next three initiatives were targeted at businesses:

4. Provide enablers to help small and medium-sized enterprises (SMEs) adopt B2B e-invoicing and payments;
5. Support vertical industry adoption of B2B e-invoicing and digital payments; and ·
6. Support the insurance industry in phasing out cheque payments to individuals.

The final two pertained to financial institutions:

7. Improve capabilities of existing clearing and settlement infrastructure necessary to implement EIP; and
8. Enable e-payment by providing incentives and supportive standards.

Experience in other countries, especially northern Europe, showed that government leadership was critical to accelerating the shift to digital payments. Indeed, no country had successfully made the transition without government intervention. Consequently, the first of the task force's four recommendations was "for the Government of Canada to lead the change by implementing electronic invoicing and payments for all government suppliers and benefit recipients." In April 2012, the federal government announced it would stop using cheques by 2016.

Working Group 2: Mobile Payments

The Mobile Payments Working Group was created when the chair of the Payments Task Force invited senior executives from the three largest retail banks and the three largest wireless carriers to a meeting in March 2011. The task force sought to encourage the development of mobile payments in Canada by creating opportunities for learning and dialogue that would enable stakeholders to create solutions to meet their own needs.

The group began on a contentious note, as the six players spent an hour resisting collaboration and trading accusations.[9] Only after a lengthy discussion (and venting session) did they agree to explore the possibility of working together to develop the next wave of mobile payments, using near-field communications (NFC).

This working group began by listening to subject matter experts from countries with experience in mobile payments. Leaders from the bank–wireless carrier joint venture in the Netherlands, French wireless carrier Orange, the GSM Association, Citibank, and the European Payments Council, along with experts in emerging retail trends, provided perspective. One of the key lessons the Mobile Payments Working Group took from its international research was the importance of collaboration.[10] Mobile payments are more likely to gain meaningful traction in a market where there is cooperation among key players – the wireless carriers, financial institutions, retailers, and service providers (both public and private).

From March to October 2011, the banks and the wireless carriers worked separately to develop a vision and principles for mobile payments. In November 2011 they came together to formulate a coordinated vision and principles they could all support:[11]

> Vision: Mobile payments in Canada will be implemented in a conve-
> nient, open, safe, and secure ecosystem supported by a standards-based
> operating framework. This framework will increase user choice and ac-
> celerate the adoption of mobile payments.
> Key principles: This framework must be open and inclusive,
> standards-based, safe and secure, responsive to consumer and mer-
> chant needs, focused, and sustainable.

Using these principles as a starting point, the six large banks and two credit union systems worked together to develop a refer-ence document for mobile payments that would enable financial institutions to begin rolling out contactless payments. This ap-proach appeared to make the most sense for Canada, which already had one of the highest penetrations of contactless terminals in the world (approximately 11 per cent of all POS terminals).[12] In May 2012 MasterCard ranked Canada second (behind Singapore) in its mobile payments readiness index, largely due to the collaboration between banks, wireless carriers, and governments fostered by the Payments Task Force. In September 2012, NFC mobile payments were introduced in Canada.

At the same time, the three largest wireless carriers (Bell, Rogers, and Telus) worked together to restructure their joint venture, EnStream, shifting its focus from competing with the banks as a mobile payments provider towards acting as a utility supporting payments made over mobile devices. They invested in a secure, standardized, and accessible service bureau to facilitate the "onboarding," transmission, and maintenance of payment and other credentials on consumers' mobile devices.[13] A conceptualized model of this utility is shown below in figure 5.1.

The EnStream utility mapped in figure 5.1 shows a mobile ecosystem that extends beyond payments providers to include service providers and governments. This concept gave the banks and wireless carriers the opportunity to think beyond the movement of value and conceive a reality where mobile phones might be used not just for payments but for many daily tasks, including health care, education, voting, and more. Creating such a system requires the ecosystem to develop and roll out standards making products and services available on all devices and wireless networks from all suppliers. While the Mobile Payments Working Group accomplished a great deal in a short time, broader industry and government engagement will be necessary to realize the full potential of the mobile ecosystem. This must include further collaboration among payment providers, wireless carriers, retailers, government services suppliers (such as health care and education), and users.

Working Group 3: Digital Identification and Authentication (DIA)

The DIA Working Group was a direct outgrowth of the Payments Roundtable "coalition of the willing." Participants, several of whom had worked on the "Own the Podium" scenario, realized

Figure 5.1: Proposed Concept for EnStream Utility to Support
the Mobile Ecosystem

Credential Issuers

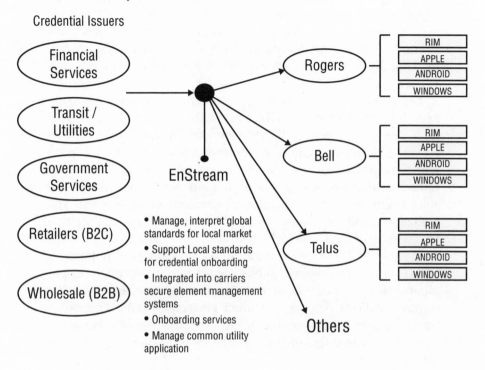

Source: EnStream, Fall 2011

the tremendous opportunity for Canada to accelerate not only its adoption of digital payments but also the growth of e-commerce and the digital delivery of government services. But this could happen only if they could resolve the biggest challenge to safe, secure, and efficient online transactions: the lack of a way to identify and authenticate the engaged parties.

Robust DIA is fundamental to digital payments. This is more than usernames and passwords: without universal strong DIA administration, Canadians' online safety and security are needlessly compromised and large segments of the economy are vulnerable to crippling attack. Trust is the essential element – trust both in attribute providers (issuers of digital identity) and in the service suppliers that rely on authenticated identity, such as banks, wireless carriers, hospitals, schools, municipalities, and provinces. The strength of that trust makes the difference between an efficient, thriving digital marketplace and one that Canadians are reluctant to participate in.[14]

The federal and provincial governments have understood the need for and challenge of DIA since 2004. As mentioned in chapter 3, the Government of British Columbia was working with the federal and other provincial governments to develop a DIA framework and infrastructure. Given the relatively small size of the Canadian marketplace, it made far more sense to build on this solid beginning than to create multiple competing systems. This realization, and the potential for public-private partnership, drove the creation of the DIA Working Group.

In early 2011, the task force facilitated meetings of representatives from the private and public sectors to develop a DIA implementation blueprint.[15] Leaders in payments, technology, wireless communications, privacy, consumer protection, and public policy gathered to form the working group, with the goal of establishing a pan-Canadian public-private digital identification and authentication regime.

This working group was one of the first to take shape after the Payments Roundtable, and it quickly established a robust membership of stakeholders eager to take part, able to make decisions, and optimistic that a pan-Canadian DIA regime was within reach. DIA also proved to be an issue of ideal size for a working group to take on: Canada's relatively small population means that there are relatively few players involved in setting standards, and it is relatively easy to get them all into a single room.[16] In fact the DIA Working Group worked so effectively together that they realized they might well outstrip public awareness and willingness to adopt, especially since for most people the idea of authentication begins and ends with passwords (and a DIA regime goes well beyond that). Users, merchants, and even governments would need to be convinced of the benefits of DIA and educated about the true costs related to privacy concerns.[17] The working group recommended the creation of a private-public DIA Council to set standards and oversee this education effort; this council was created in 2013.

Working Group 4: Self-Governing Organization

As described in the previous chapter, the task force asked the "coalition of the willing" to form a working group to develop the mandate, membership, governance, and operational organization of the self-governing organization (SGO) overseeing the payments ecosystem. The SGO Working Group was chaired by a senior executive from the largest Canadian bank and included representation from the two largest banks; the Canadian Bankers Association; networks (both regulated and unregulated); PayPal (a new entrant); corporate, small, and medium-sized businesses; and retail users.

The SGO Working Group fleshed out the mandate, governance, and operational structure according to the action plan and timeline developed in a Strategy Testing Workshop in February 2011 (see table 5.1). This action plan addressed interim funding and human resources, questions of legal form, a permanent membership-based funding model, and strategies for identifying individuals to govern and lead the SGO. It also developed an outreach and member engagement strategy designed to build recognition, engage potential members, and test and confirm the SGO's mandate, governance, and operating and funding models.

Experts Refined the Proposed Governance Framework

After testing the Proposed Governance Framework with the Payments Roundtable, the task force prepared a discussion paper – *The Way We Pay* – which was posted on its website with questions and suggestions to stimulate ideas, as well as a request for comments. This request generated many submissions from stakeholders and members of the public offering detailed comments and concerns about the implementation of this radical new approach to governing the payments industry.

From February to October 2011, the Payments Task Force and the SGO Working Group worked closely with three expert advisory groups to flesh out the Proposed Governance Framework and

Table 5.1 Timeline and Actions for the SGO Working Group (from Feb. 2011 workshop)

Completion Date	Actions
Feb. 2011	Establish SGO Working Group.
March 2011	In conjunction with Payments Task Force interim report, publicize concept of SGO Framework.
Early spring 2011	Develop working prototype; flesh out details of how SGO will work in practice (relation to other framework components and to existing structures).
Late spring 2011	Establish concept-validated board structure, operational structure, role, funding; identify initial agenda; set plans and engage a wider range of stakeholders.
June 2011	Start operation "training wheels" (pilot); establish skeleton staffing and provisional funding. Get the prototype up and running (will help "sell" broader roll-out).
Sept. 2011	Go/no-go for SGO. Hand off from task force – transfer of working group.
Dec. 2011	Task force report – endorse SGO.
2012	Launch SGO and supporting regulatory, legislative changes. Leverage 2012 review of financial institution statutes.

address the issues raised by these comments and discussions. These advisory groups performed the targeted analysis required to resolve uncertainties, as well as determining the nature and form of any additional analysis required.

1. The *Consumer Advisory Group* developed and refined a set of principles both users and suppliers believed were fundamental to any successful payments system: *trust, access,* and *good value.* The task force adopted these principles as the heart of a new governance model. This advisory group was chaired by a marketing executive from the private sector and composed of five consumer advocates (representing a variety of consumer groups) and five marketing executives, along with task force representatives.

2. The mandate of the *Regulatory Advisory Group* was to determine whether legislation was required to implement the governance model and, if so, whether the federal government was able to pass such legislation under the Canadian constitution. A review

of existing legislation identified some significant gaps in the current Canadian legislative regime. More worrisome was the lack of an overarching framework to provide coherence and responsiveness in dealing with a changing environment. One of the most important gaps was that new players in the payments industry, such as PayPal, Apple, and Google, were subject to no oversight at all. Another was the lack of transparency and clear disclosure regarding consumer risks and protections. Such problems would only increase as the Canadian payments system evolved.

The Regulatory Advisory Group recommended and outlined legislation to define the payments industry as a distinct sector and to spell out the way in which participants in the payments system would be identified. Further goals of the legislation would be to provide for a principles-based oversight function and to allow recognition of a self-governing organization (or organizations) to which authority could be delegated. This advisory group was chaired by an economics professor emeritus and composed of four economists and eight lawyers (including constitutional, competition, and payments experts), again supported by members of the task force.

3. The mandate of the *Governance Advisory Group* was to test the proposed governance model and provide guidance on the mandate and operation of the Payments Oversight Body, the self-governing organization, and the core infrastructure provider. This advisory group was chaired by a senior legal counsellor with extensive board experience. It also included a former chair of the Ontario Securities Commission, a former deputy governor of the Bank of Canada, the president and CEO of the Canadian Payments Association, a deputy superintendent of financial institutions, the senior bank executive chairing the SGO Working Group, and the chair of the Payments Task Force.

The advisory groups also met with each other with some regularity, and interesting developments arose from this cross-pollination. For example, the Consumer Advisory Group met with the Regulatory Advisory Group to discuss the principles underpinning the governance process. While the Consumer Advisory Group was concerned with issues such as fairness, the Regulatory Advisory Group was focused on the enforceability of principles-based legislation.

Through facilitated dialogue and several sessions together, the two groups were able to find language to address their concerns.

Similarly, the Consumer Advisory Group met with the Payments to Individuals Subcommittee of the EIP Working Group to discuss the implementation of eliminating cheque payments to individuals. The Payments to Individuals Subcommittee was focused on eliminating cheque payments as quickly as possible, while the Consumer Advisory Group was concerned about ensuring an approach that considered customer needs, especially those of the technologically disadvantaged.

From March to October 2011, the SGO Working Group and the three advisory groups developed a detailed roadmap to build an effective governance framework for the Canadian payments industry. In November, the Payments Task Force took all the work that had been done and communicated it through the following four policy papers:

1. The rationale (*Users and Their Discontent*)
2. The governance model (*Stakeholders and Their Disconnect*)
3. Necessary legislation (*Establishing the Payments Industry*), and
4. Required infrastructure (*A Reinvented CPA*)

Although the payments industry clearly existed in the minds of the Roundtable, working group, and advisory group participants, it did not exist in legislation. Nor did stakeholders, especially users and new entrants, have a role in governing the industry. And the antiquated clearing and payments infrastructure was inaccessible to new entrants. The new SGO promised to be a key step in addressing these challenges.

Setback for the SGO

But the SGO did not go forward. In part this was because SGO Working Group members from the banking sector withdrew their support. These individuals had not participated in the Payments Roundtable. They had not seen how new technology and entrants would disrupt the traditional payments arena. Rather than seeing the SGO as an opportunity to use their substantial influence over the system to ensure that the banking industry continued to play a key role in the future payments world, the banks apparently preferred to retain the status quo for as long as possible.

Having lost the support of the largest banks, members of the SGO Working Group decided in October 2011 that they could not create an organization without specific instructions from the Minister of Finance. Had the Finance Minister green-lighted the creation of a payments SGO at this time, it would have been easy to roll the working and advisory groups into the organization. The initiatives outlined by the working groups would have progressed much faster with the SGO's support and oversight, especially since clear roadmaps to achieve their objectives had already been prepared. The advisory groups would have become standing committees of the SGO, working with government on legislative and regulatory issues. One of the most pressing issues was the need to work with consumer groups, provincial governments, and the Department of Finance to create an overarching consumer protection framework. In addition, the standing committees would support standards development and consumer education for new products and services.

In hindsight, we now realize that the Payments Task Force missed an opportunity. In February 2011, at the final workshop, it was clear that the Roundtable saw itself as the beginning of a payments industry SGO. They recommended a payments council of forty to sixty members (the same size as the Roundtable) and clearly endorsed the proposed governance model. Had the task force engaged the entire Payments Roundtable and other key players to form the SGO Working Group at that point, it would have created a group firmly committed to the creation of a more inclusive payments industry and have captured the creativity and enthusiasm shown in the last Roundtable workshop. Instead, the working group was assembled from a smaller group of about ten people, only about half of whom had been part of the Roundtable process. Many of these participants were not persuaded of the need for governance changes and were not prepared to support the SGO.

Working Group 5: Payment Processing, Clearing, and Settlement Infrastructure

The Automated Clearing and Settlement System (ACSS) that handles most transactions was implemented in the early 1980s, and it is showing its age. Access is limited, finality of payments does not occur for over twenty-four hours, and end-to-end processing of payments is slow. Consumers increasingly question why it takes three days to pay a utility bill when they can send a text message in seconds. The Large Value Transfer System (LVTS) used by banks and governments was built in 1999. It, too, would benefit from technological enhancements allowing it to clear and settle both retail and wholesale payments more efficiently.

The design, governance, and operation of this crucial infrastructure has created barriers to entry for new participants and has hampered the innovation needed to create digital payments services and realize the principles of *trust, access,* and *good value*[18] so vital to the future of the Canadian payments system. Moreover, little consideration was being given to the critical issue of interoperability with the payments systems of other countries. These core national payment clearing and settlement systems needed to be upgraded.

When first approached about this working group, the large banks that effectively control this infrastructure were not willing to work with the task force to resolve these issues. Consequently, the task force started worked with a few individuals familiar with these systems to develop recommendations regarding core payments infrastructure. Shortly before the task force's mandate expired at the end of 2011, the banks began participating in meetings, listening to presentations by infrastructure suppliers, and discussing possible ways to evolve the infrastructure to meet current and future requirements. With more time to work together, this working group likely would have developed a roadmap for action to upgrade the payments infrastructure. Nonetheless, as described below, the CPA has continued to make progress on the task force's recommendations.

Recommendations to the Finance Minister

Based on the output from the working and advisory groups, the task force made four recommendations to the Minister of Finance[19] for the government to lead the way in transitioning to digital payments. These recommendations are outlined in box 5.2.

Box 5.2: Task Force Recommendations to the Minister of Finance

RECOMMENDATIONS: GOVERNMENT MUST LEAD
THE CHANGE

For Canada's payment system to substantially modernize, changes are required in multiple arenas, from consumer behaviours to accounting solutions to the very procedures governments rely upon in delivering services. Industry has not implemented change, in part because of uncertainty and lack of coordination. Therefore, the Government of Canada should lead the change by undertaking the following actions:

- Implement electronic invoicing and payments (EIP) for all government suppliers and recipients of benefits.
- Partner with the private sector to create a mobile ecosystem.
- Propel the building of a digital identification and authentication (DIA) regime to underpin a modernized payments system and protect Canadians' privacy.
- Overhaul the governance, business model, and powers of the Canadian Payments Association and transform the payments infrastructure so that it can innovate to meet the evolving needs of Canadians in a digital economy.

Source: Task Force for the Payments System Review, *Moving Canada into the Digital Age*, page 5
Reproduced with the permission of the Department of Finance, 2015: http://payment-systemreview.ca/wp-content/themes/psr-esp-hub/documents/rf_eng.pdf

These recommendations arose from the conviction that if government took the lead in making changes, with support from stakeholders, this would catalyse the larger changes needed to realize the potential of the digital economy. As a major user of the payments system, the administrative arm of government could make changes in its operations – in EIP, mobile, and DIA – that would drive wider adoption, encourage alignment among sectors, and provide the necessary momentum for industry to follow suit.

Progress since the Conclusion of the Payments Task Force

Overall, the payments system has come a long way since the task force made its recommendations in March 2012. The Department of Public Works and Government Services responded quickly to the task force's first recommendation, promising to eliminate federal government cheques by April 2016. It was difficult to find a federal government sponsor for the mobile ecosystem, but the marketplace has accelerated the adoption of mobile payments and other services. The federal government, through Treasury Board Secretariat, continued to support the creation of a digital identification and authentication regime. Finally, the Finance Minister tabled legislation to overhaul the governance of the Canadian Payments Association.

As detailed below, the federal government has ratified, disseminated, and begun to act upon most of the measures developed through the task force process. This is the fifth step in the catalytic governance model.

The Canadian Payments System Has Evolved Rapidly ...

Significant progress has been made on all four of the Payments Task Force's recommendations to move the Canadian payments system into the digital age.

1. Implement Electronic Invoicing and Payments (EIP)

The first recommendation was for governments to fully automate the end-to-end processing of payables and receivables by implementing electronic invoicing and payments. Not only would this save our economy $7.7 billion in annual costs and improve the nation's productivity, it would also lay the foundation for much bigger savings – the 1 per cent to 2 per cent of GDP (or between $16 billion and $32 billion annually) that countries like Sweden, Denmark, and Finland are realizing through automated public and private sector service delivery, which is enabled by EIP.

More than 15 per cent of all invoices in the European Union are now sent and paid electronically, with Scandinavian countries at the forefront. Developing countries such as Brazil, Mexico, India, and China are also automating the processing of receivables and payables. On the other hand, Canadian banks continue to process almost 1 billion cheques annually and are investing hundreds of millions of dollars into imaging technology to capture obsolete pieces of paper. Corporations and institutions are reluctant to make the necessary investments in accounting systems and processes for EIP without common standards and infrastructure to carry the remittance information. This is in part why Canada's productivity and competitiveness continue to decline relative to that of the northern European leaders.[20]

Shortly after the Minister of Finance released the task force report in March 2012, the Minister of Public Works and Government Services (PWGSC) announced that the federal government would be eliminating payments by cheque to citizens and businesses by April 2016. PWGSC's director general for Banking and Cash Management had led two of the Payments Task Force's EIP subcommittees – Payments to Individuals and Payments to Large Corporations and Governments. From 2011 to autumn 2013, she developed and began implementing a plan to deliver on the promise of phasing out cheques.

PWGSC promoted[21] direct debit and online bill payments to Canadians and their financial services suppliers. In March 2012, they issued a request for information for prepaid cards to replace cheque payments to recipients of benefits who were unable or unwilling to share their banking information with the government. And in October 2013, they released a request for information for a portal to support small and medium-sized enterprises sending invoices and receiving payments electronically to and from governments. This portal must be sufficiently scalable to support payments to all governments (federal, provincial, and municipal) and possibly all B2B (business-to-business) payments. PWGSC has indicated that it will be seeking proposals to build and operate the business-to-government (B2G) portal in 2015. At the same time, a number of large corporations have created their own portals, which they require their small and medium-sized suppliers to use. These actions are accelerating EIP adoption in Canada.

Standards are essential for EIP to work seamlessly from organization to organization. The Standards Subcommittee of the Payments Task Force, led by the Canadian Payments Association (CPA), concluded that Canada would be best served by adopting a new benchmark – that of the International Organization for Standardization: ISO 20022. These standards support the transmission of large data, are neutral to allow for new entrants, and align with international standards. In October 2011 the CPA board approved the adoption of ISO 20022, and in 2013, the CPA worked with its members to accelerate the timeline for implementation of this standard.

The CPA is also working on a technology roadmap to improve the Automated Clearing and Settlement System and the Large Value Transfer System to provide the transaction information necessary to reconcile accounts when an automated payment is received. So far, these efforts to update the systems have made little headway, given the financial institutions' preference to go slowly.

2. Create a Mobile Ecosystem

At a Mobile Payments Working Group meeting in June 2011, the banks and wireless carriers committed to launch the first mobile payments app in Canada by July 2012. In fall of that year a bank (CIBC) and a wireless carrier (Rogers) met the challenge, conducting the first mobile NFC (proximity) payment in Canada. Since then five of the six large banks, Desjardins Group, and a handful of smaller players (including President's Choice and Peoples Trust) have launched mobile payments with at least one carrier (either a mobile payment app or through their mobile banking app). Mobile payment capability is now available to about 40 per cent of Canadians.

Because most arrangements between banks and wireless carriers are bilateral, however, mobile payments are only available on a few handsets, operating systems, and networks. This fragmented approach and the lack of common standards has slowed the rollout of mobile payments to wireless carriers and handsets running on open operating systems such as Android.[22]

Merchant terminals in Canada are increasingly NFC enabled, especially those in high-volume locations (such as grocery and convenience stores, gas stations, and coffee shops). The combination of bank-wireless carrier offers and NFC penetration makes Canada a leader in mobile payments among developed countries.[23] Canada is currently the only country that offers debit and credit card credentials on mobile phones. However, these are mobile-enabled card payments, not immediate funds transfers from point-to-point.

It is important to note that the mobile ecosystem is more than payments. It represents the ability of citizens to gain access to both public and private sector services anywhere, anytime, in real time. Services such as renewing a driver's licence, viewing the results of a blood test, checking school attendance or grades, voting in a municipal election, checking into a flight or a hotel room or an office, getting on the subway, or downloading a book from the library should be as simple to manage as "tap and go." The next step in building this mobile ecosystem is to collaborate on digital identification and authentication, plus the standards and consumer education necessary to make this vision a reality.

3. Build a Digital Identification and Authentication Regime

Implementation of the Payments Task Force's recommendation to build a digital identification and authentication regime is also moving forward. In 2013, a small group of government, bank, and wireless carrier executives established the Digital Identification and Authentication Council of Canada (DIACC), with Aran Hamilton acting as interim president.

By the end of 2014, the DIACC had about forty member organizations and a mailing list of more than 2,000 individuals. Using standards adopted by the DIACC, the Province of British Columbia (BC) has been rolling out digital identity cards (BC Services) since spring 2013. Other provinces, such as Ontario and Nova Scotia, are considering joining them. In September 2014, the DIACC successfully demonstrated that a bank account could be opened online in less than five minutes (as compared with the minimum thirty minutes required in a bank branch). It is now working on a proof of concept for the health-care industry and a roll-out plan to enrol consumers in gaining access to these services.

In 2015, the DIACC's priority is to prove that digital ID and authentication can work for all Canadians and to roll out changes to the regulatory environments across Canada. Next steps include:

- developing a business model for rolling out and operating a Canadian identity platform that serves the needs of all users and stakeholders and secures Canada's place in the global digital economy;
- identifying and publishing protocol specifications or standards that outline how organizations should protect identity transactions; and
- engaging citizens in conversations about digital identity through innovative projects and open dialogue.

4. Pass Legislation to Overhaul the Governance of the Payments Industry

The task force's report also called for an overhaul in the governance of payments that would prioritize users' needs, protect the public interest, and encourage collaboration and innovation among all stakeholders. In particular, the report called for defining payments as an industry and requiring all members of the payments community – from service providers to merchants and users – to become members of an industry association. This broad-based, collaborative, self-governance organization would have a new public oversight body. Government would also need to reinvent the objectives, governance, powers, business model, and funding of the Canadian Payments Association (CPA) so that the CPA could deliver the modern infrastructure required to meet the payments needs of all Canadians into the future.

On the basis of this report, in March 2012 the Minister of Finance announced plans to review the governance framework for the payments system. He also established the Finance Canada Payments Consultative Committee (FinPay) to help the government stay abreast of market developments and to contribute to policy development in support of an innovative and safe payments system. Public and private sector stakeholders were invited to join the committee, and the inaugural meeting took place in the summer of 2012. The minister also confirmed that the code of conduct for the credit and debit card industry in Canada was being reviewed to ensure that it guides the development of mobile payments in Canada.

On 11 March 2014 the Finance Minister announced his intention to strengthen the governance of Canada's payments sector. By December 2014, these efforts had culminated in significant legislation affecting the Canadian Payments Association. This legislation made the CPA more accountable and ensured that it follows corporate governance best practices.[24] The Finance Minister's expanded oversight and directive powers are designed to ensure that the CPA provides the modern systems required to meet Canadians' payments needs. The legislation also introduced changes to the Payment Clearing and Settlement Act to improve the Bank of Canada's oversight of retail payments systems. These changes took place with remarkable speed: less than two years after the task force's report, the government had introduced and passed legislation and was beginning to implement it.

... but Revolutionary Change Will Be Necessary

All these changes are significant. They do a great deal to move Canada's payments system forward, and they represent speedy action when measured against the usual pace of regulatory change. In less turbulent times, this quick progress would be remarkable.

Nevertheless, even though the Canadian payments system has evolved significantly, it is not keeping up with the monumental shifts in the global environment. The technological revolution continues to accelerate, driven mostly by advances and innovations on the part of tech companies and other new entrants. New features in smart devices and product innovations emerge almost daily, and these are disrupting old systems and changing the payments landscape at a breathtaking pace.

For example, in September 2014 Apple announced it was launching its own mobile payment platform. Dubbed Apple Pay, the system allows iPhone users to purchase goods at hundreds of thousands of retail locations by simply holding the smart phone near a cashier terminal. In the past, two major hurdles have hampered mobile payments offerings: acceptance and security. By partnering with retailers like Macy's and restaurants like McDonald's, as well as the three major credit card companies, Apple is addressing the challenge of acceptance.

Apple is also taking an innovative approach to dealing with security. By combining an NFC-enabled phone with fingerprint recognition, Apple can be almost certain users are who they say they are. In addition Apple knows a whole lot more – users' locations, the stores they frequent – that will assist them in detecting fraud. Because of this approach to authentication and highly secure protection of card numbers, Apple was able to convince the networks that it provided consumers with superior security and privacy.[25]

Most observers agree that Apple represents the thin end of the wedge. With 800 million of the 2 billion credit card holders globally already registered in the Apple (iTunes) wallet, and a similar number using the Google operating system,[26] many experts expect these companies to dominate mobile payments in five to ten years.

Several other necessary developments are not taking place because they require intensive collaboration among incumbents, new entrants, and users. For instance, consumers increasingly expect immediate access to information, to payments, and to their funds – but current clearing and settlement systems (ACSS and LVTS) are unable to meet such expectations. Bringing these systems in line with the demands of the digital age is not a matter of incremental fixes or evolution: they must be entirely rebuilt. Such an endeavour requires industry-wide collaboration on standards, customer education, and consumer protection. This has not happened. Similarly, resolving the debit/credit card issue, establishing standards to accelerate the roll-out of electronic invoicing and payments, and creating a mobile ecosystem all require broad-based collaboration.

Canada has not created an inclusive and collaborative governance model for payments because government and incumbents believe that allowing a gradual evolution of the payments system will be less disruptive than embracing the transition to digital payments and a digital economy. In effect they have opted for evolution, not revolution.

This can be seen in the governance legislation implemented in December 2014. The legislation significantly improved the independence and accountability of the Canadian Payments Association. However, it was targeted at regulated financial institutions, which are only one part of the new payments industry.[27] By not recognizing "payments" as an industry and not creating an industry governing body, the legislation fails to support the inclusiveness and collaboration that will be necessary to build a digital payments system. It does not guarantee new entrants access to the system or guide their behaviour within it. It does not encourage consumer acceptance or ensure consumers' protection. It is not sufficiently flexible and adaptable to keep up with the rapid and continuous changes in the industry. In our view, it will not be effective in governing payments in the information age.

The catalytic governance model provides an approach that is more likely than other methods to be successful in dealing with such challenges. By engaging all of the relevant stakeholders in ongoing dialogue focused on understanding changes to the system and co-creating the desired future, it facilitates collaboration and adaptation to change.

A Look at the Future

Leading the world in payments – truly "Owning the Podium" – requires revolutionary changes in both technology and governance of the payments system. The technological transformation is well under way, but the governance system is not creating the conditions for the collaboration and rapid, responsive learning that are required.

In fact, of the four plausible futures developed by the Roundtable, the scenario that best describes our current reality is "Tech-tonic Shift": rapid adoption of technology and minimal alignment and collaboration. (See http://paymentsystemreview.ca/wp-content/themes/psr-esp-hub/documents/r01_eng.pdf; a brief summary is also available in the appendix of this volume.) This scenario projects one of the least desirable outcomes for Canadians and their financial institutions, with a series of disruptions on the part of "tech titans" creating a fragmented and messy payments environment. The scenario projects a dramatic shift of payments away from financial institutions and towards new entrants, with technology companies like Apple and Google providing most payment services to consumers and SMEs by the year 2020.

Recent events, such as the rapid introduction and adoption of Apple Pay, seem drawn directly from the Tech-tonic Shift projections. It is clear that the old payments system is being replaced increasingly and rapidly by innovative new entrants. It is also likely that these changes in the context of a rapidly changing and largely ungoverned payments industry will result in a major crisis or disruption.

The Tech-tonic Shift scenario also provides some guideposts for how Canada might deal with this increasingly fragmented environment. It imagines that in 2021 – after a series of major disruptions to the payments industry – a deputy minister of finance writes a memorandum to the finance minister calling for a new Payments Task Force and outlining a number of issues this task force would need to address, including:

1. whether and how best to complete the phase-out of cash and cheques;
2. what options are available to reduce online fraud and strengthen digital identification and authentication;
3. how to improve public understanding of the payments system;

4. what possibilities are available for more effective collection of
   tax online; and
5. how to streamline the payments system and reduce overall
   costs to users.

Such a memo suggests what we have come to believe over the
course of this effort, and what the Governance Framework recommended
by the Payments Task Force also recognized: that the
payments system will continue to be subject to rapid, constant,
discontinuous changes, and that addressing those realities will require
an inclusive and learning-based approach to governance of
the industry. It will require the whole payments industry – suppliers,
incumbents, new entrants, and users – to collaborate. It means
forming a collaborative self-governing organization and giving it
the power to engage in inclusive dialogue, develop a vision of
plausible futures, and co-create the desired future.

In short, it will require a process of catalytic governance.

In the next chapter we step back from the Payments Task Force
and look more broadly at leadership and governance in the information
age and at the lessons we have learned, and use that overview
to develop a more detailed model of catalytic governance. We
hope this model can be applied more widely to resolve wicked
problems and to meet the challenges of leadership and governance
in the information age.

chapter six

Lessons Learned and the Catalytic Governance Model

In this chapter we summarize the lessons we have learned and elaborate a more detailed model of catalytic governance that can be applied to other wicked problems we face today. The lessons we have learned are both specific to the Payments Task Force and of broader, more general relevance.

Specific Lessons

We learned several important lessons from the work of the Payments Task Force and Roundtable:

Canada needs a digital payments strategy: Without a digital payments system, it will be difficult for Canada to fully participate in the global digital economy. Such a system must include: a digital identification and authentication regime; reliable, affordable broadband access; a trustworthy, accessible, and low-cost system to transfer and store critical information; and an effective and inclusive governance mechanism. Without these, Canadians will be unable to fully engage in the digital economy of the twenty-first century, with negative consequences for our standard of living and international competitiveness. Moreover, a thoroughly digitized payments system could help save the Canadian economy as much as 2 per cent of GDP in productivity gains, equivalent to $32 billion in annual savings.[1] Even more important, such a Canadian payments system would lead to far greater choice, efficiency, and convenience for consumers, businesses, governments, and organizations, as well as a safer, more secure system.

Expand the dialogue through online engagement and social media: Online engagement has a great deal of potential to facilitate public and stakeholder discussions of this kind. Finding effective means of doing so will be crucial in future efforts to develop a more inclusive and dialogue-based process of governance. The work of the task force in engaging broader publics both online and in other ways was an important step forward relative to what had been done before; however, much more is needed.

Trust the process: Another critical lesson we learned was the importance of trusting the process and continually widening the circle of engagement. Although the task force based its Proposed Governance Model (discussed in chapter 4) on the process of the Payments Roundtable, it failed to follow through. Rather than handing the SGO over to the "coalition of the willing" emerging from the Roundtable and continuing to widen the circle from there, the task force reverted to a more traditional notion of governance and turned the development of the SGO over to a narrower working group with representation by category. Nor did it insist that the members be individuals who had participated in the Roundtable process.

The importance of government participation: The effectiveness of the Roundtable was diminished by the decision of senior government officials not to participate directly in its work. In a more traditional context this decision makes sense as a way to protect the independence of the task force and the decision-making prerogatives of a minister of finance. But because of the way the Roundtable operated – as a dialogue in which members participated in their own right rather than as representatives – there was little threat to that independence or those prerogatives. This is underlined by the fact that a senior official of the Bank of Canada was a full member of the Roundtable without undermining either the independence of the effort or the prerogatives of his institution.

Nevertheless, because senior government officials did not participate in the journey, they did not benefit from the exponential learning opportunity created by the Payments Roundtable. When the report landed on their desks in 2012, they needed to study it and the payments industry for another two years – only to ultimately come to similar conclusions as those the task force had reached. Legislation took another year. Because of this delay, the payments community will have to figure out how to re-create an SGO, the core elements of which had already been created in the working and advisory groups overseen by the task force.

Rethink commissions and task forces: The work of most commissions and task forces ends with the creation of a report. Such recommendations are useful and important, but wicked problems demand more than recommendations – they require action. Rather than simply studying problems and proposing solutions, task forces can lay the groundwork for action on those solutions if they have a mandate, resources, and commitment from the decision-making body, as well as adequate stakeholder engagement in the process.

This represents a dramatic shift in how governments (and boards) operate and make decisions in a turbulent environment. Governments would need to clearly define the issue and the acceptable boundaries for the solution. They would need to ensure that key stakeholders are engaged in the process and establish checkpoints to adjust the mandate and boundary conditions as needed. And they would need to be prepared to conduct their work in parallel to task forces, not just after receiving the report.

General Lessons

Effective leadership and governance in the information age depend less and less on traditional, top-down approaches and more and more on creating shared meanings and frameworks. This process of deeper learning engages government, stakeholders, and the public to catalyse action. That, in essence, is what the Payments Task Force did.

We came to understand that what is most important is the continuing process of dialogue and learning that allows people to construct shared mental maps, norms, and expectations. Within this framework, a wide range of players can innovate and act on a succession of initiatives – an emergent strategy – to deal with rapidly changing issues. This catalytic process is key to the kinds of leadership and governance we need in the information age. *Catalytic governance is a process for leading transformative change that engages a wide range of stakeholders in dialogue and empowers them to develop and enact a vision of a desired future.* It is a process that is more open, collaborative, forward-looking, and action-oriented than traditional approaches.

In the past, most systems of governance have been controlled by relatively small and homogeneous elites with similar belief systems, upbringings, and social class. Whatever agreement was reached by these elites was accepted by the larger society as legitimate and could be acted on effectively. Most of our governance systems are still designed to operate in this top-down manner, on the basis of "elite accommodation."

But the information age requires that we engage more stakeholders with diverse backgrounds and interests, and the issues we now face cut across many boundaries (national, jurisdictional, organizational, and more). Moreover the speed, complexity, and interconnectedness of change mean we can no longer separate planning and action in the traditional way.

The catalytic governance model emphasizes that a wider range of stakeholders needs to be involved in the governance process in the information age, and that governments, boards, and other governing bodies need to make room for these players. This means that governments and boards need to relax day-to-day control (or the illusion of such control) and shift to a catalytic role focusing on:

- framing issues and the agenda;
- using their convening power to ensure that a full range of stakeholders and perspectives are engaged in addressing those issues;
- defining the rules of engagement;

- encouraging stakeholders to explore different perspectives and alternative futures and to look for common ground;
- participating in (or at least monitoring) the learning process of those stakeholders in order to be able to quickly understand the outcome, anticipate problems, and respond without delay;
- ratifying and disseminating the mental maps and strategy created by this learning process; and
- acting and encouraging action on the emerging strategic direction (including legislating if necessary).

In the information age we urgently require catalytic governance practices that enable people from diverse backgrounds and interests to work through issues, find common ground, construct shared mental maps and a vision of the future, and begin to act on that basis. As we have seen, the Payments Task Force provides a rich case study of one such effort.

The Catalytic Role of the Payments Task Force

Traditional notions of governance and decision making tend to be relatively simple: issues arise, key interests advocate different responses, and decisions are made. This may work well enough when the issues and the possible responses are reasonably well understood, and where those involved share similar assumptions, language, background, and culture. But when, as is increasingly common today, the nature of the issues and the possible responses are unclear, and when people with very different beliefs, problem-definitions, values, or traditions must find common ground as a basis for collaborative action, a different process is needed. That is where the catalytic role of the Payments Task Force comes in. The task force:

- created a space for dialogue and learning with stakeholders and others in the governance process;
- engaged a wide range of stakeholders (incumbents, new entrants, and users) in dialogue, and worked with them to confirm and further develop the initial framing of the issue;

- explored alternative perspectives on the future of the payments system using scenarios;
- focused on discovering common ground (of which there was more than most had expected) and used that as a foundation for co-creating a shared mental map of the desired future;
- drew on that mental map to guide a process of experimental actions and action learning and to test new ways forward;
- evolved a strategic direction and initial steps to implement it, and highlighted these in its final report.

A key to using such a dialogue-based process is to recognize that it does not replace debate, advocacy, negotiation, or decision making; it precedes them. Dialogue creates the shared language and framework, the foundation for new processes and institutions, and the mutual trust and understanding that enable subsequent debate, negotiation, decision making, and collaborative action to be more productive, and to require less time. In today's world, we need to make room for real dialogue from the outset and throughout many of our most important decision-making processes, and to do so in a more explicit and systematic way. Such an investment of time and effort to get key stakeholders onto the same page is essential if we are to respond quickly and effectively to the maelstrom of change we face in the information age.

This approach differed from traditional governance and decision making in several ways. It used *dialogue* to uncover assumptions, share and broaden perspectives, find common ground, and build community. And it used *scenarios* to anchor its learning process, focusing the dialogue on alternative possible futures, challenging assumptions about what the future might hold, exploring uncertainties, reframing risks and opportunities, developing and stress-testing strategies, and finding common ground.

As we saw, the results were striking. Those who initially identified primarily as bankers, or tech executives, or wireless carriers, or retailers – or in other ways – gradually came to see themselves as part of a more inclusive payments industry. Prior to the work of the task force and Roundtable no such awareness and no such industry existed. Today this awareness is alive and well, and we see more and more stakeholders acting in ways consistent with that new understanding. This is how new mental maps are formed and how transformative change happens.

Traditional Models of Public Decision Making

Because it operates at arm's length from government, a task force or commission is well positioned to create a space for dialogue and learning in which politicking can be suspended.[2] But doing so goes well beyond the traditional role that a task force or commission is expected to play (namely, to study an issue, receive submissions, and make expert recommendations).[3] The Payments Task Force quickly ran up against these more traditional models of public decision making and expectations of the role a task force should play.

The "Decisionist" Model

Usually ascribed to Max Weber, the "Decisionist" model assumes that public policymakers are the group most competent to make judgments on policy ends. Experts provide advice about how best to achieve these policy ends, and politicians then act on that advice. A good example is the development of a government's budget.

The Decisionist model predominates, for example, in Westminster systems of government (such as Canada's) based on the principle of ministerial responsibility. Guided (and limited) by this traditional model, Canadian government officials were slow both to understand what the task force was trying to accomplish and to act on the opportunities it created, even though delay meant forgoing billions of dollars in savings and limiting Canada's full participation in the global digital economy. The Decisionist framework also informed officials' reluctance to participate directly in the learning process of the task force and its Roundtable: in their view, participation threatened to undermine the decision-making prerogatives of the minister.

Figure 6.1: The "Decisionist" Model

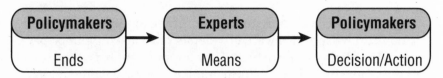

The "Technocratic" Model

The "Technocratic" model can be traced back to Henri de Saint-Simon and Francis Bacon. Its proponents argue that most policy problems are so complex and unprecedented that politicians alone cannot determine policy ends. Instead, experts are needed to make judgments about policy ends as well as the most effective means of achieving them, and politicians act based on these recommendations. A good example is national regulation of health or environmental standards.

The Technocratic model predominates in many of the organizations that sent members to the Roundtable – in particular, banks and other large financial institutions. This made it more difficult for these organizations to understand and act upon the lessons learned through the Payments Task Force process. As a result, for example, these institutions were unable to see the value of establishing a self-governing organization (SGO) that included a wide range of stakeholders whose expertise they did not accept – and equally unable to understand that not acting held even greater risks.

Figure 6.2: The "Technocratic" Model

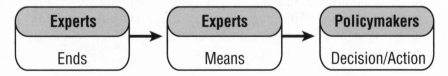

Drawbacks of the Traditional Models

The traditional Decisionist and Technocratic models have several serious drawbacks. They are non-democratic: lacking public participation, dialogue, or debate. They are prone to bias: the views of those not sharing the political opinion or ethical values of policymakers/experts are frequently dismissed, and the real reasons for policy prescriptions are often opaque. And they ignore perspectives of those outside the circle of insiders and experts. Limiting the players and perspectives engaged in the decision-making process also limits understanding of the broad context of the issue under review. When they do not engage different perspectives, participants are less likely to challenge their own assumptions, or even to be aware that others may hold very different assumptions about the questions at issue. This limits the scope for learning and dialogue.

More generally, the rapid and discontinuous change we now face cannot be adequately addressed by the slow and linear approach to policy and strategy of the traditional models. Effective leadership and governance in the information age require more.

Democratizing the Traditional Model: The "Pragmatic" Model

The development of the "Pragmatic" model represented an important step towards a more inclusive and dialogue-based approach to public decision making. Jürgen Habermas, drawing on the work of John Dewey, George Herbert Mead, Charles Sanders Pierce, and other Pragmatist philosophers, introduced this model.[4]

It argues that policy ends and means can be effectively determined in a rational discourse among experts, policymakers, and the public. Such a discourse – following rules that are formal, rational, and fair – can develop both new policy ends and the means to implement them, based on explicit and widely debated values and societal needs. The Pragmatic model supports pluralism, "deliberative democracy," and a more democratic control of expertise in policy.

Figure 6.3: The "Pragmatic" Model

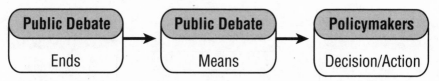

The Catalytic Governance Model

The "Catalytic Governance" model represents an important further step, moving from theory to practice. This approach – developed and tested through the task force process – is inclusive, dialogue-based, forward-looking, and action-oriented. It is designed for the interconnected and rapidly changing world of the information age.

Using the experience and detailed case analysis contained in earlier chapters, we can begin to elaborate such a Catalytic Governance model. This model has five steps, which are summarized in figure 6.4 and elaborated in the paragraphs that follow.

Step 1: Frame the Problem and Set Boundaries for Solutions

The first step in the catalytic governance process is for governments or boards (or others with policy responsibility) to determine whether the process is needed in the first place. Simpler issues will not require such a large investment of time and resources and can be addressed through traditional approaches. But when the nature of both the issues and the possible responses is unclear, when the issue is a "wicked problem," and when people with very different beliefs, problem definitions, values, or traditions must find common ground as a basis for collaborative action, a catalytic governance process is required.

In those circumstances, governments or boards take the initial step of framing the problem and the agenda, defining the catalytic governance process to be followed and the range of stakeholders

Figure 6.4: The "Catalytic Governance" Model, Revisited

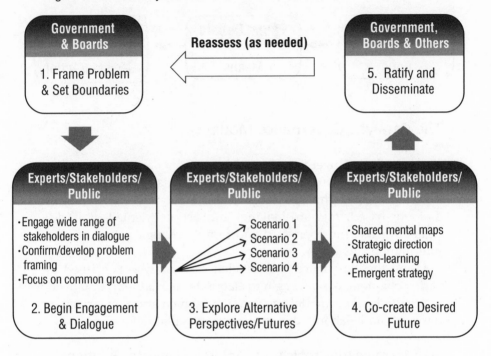

to be included, and setting the boundaries for acceptable solutions. Above all, they need to be prepared to trust the process, and to place the onus on the stakeholders involved to deliver an acceptable outcome.

Step 2: Begin Engagement and Dialogue

The second step in the process is to begin to engage a wide range of stakeholders around the issue, embedding the ground rules of dialogue and engagement in all conversations from the outset. Governing bodies need to ensure that all the key stakeholder viewpoints are included in the process, including those normally underrepresented. The stakeholders should be selected to be a microcosm of the system at issue, not just representatives of particular interests. In a true dialogue, participants need to be free to speak for themselves, not as representatives. A continuing and expanding process of dialogue and engagement is fundamental to catalytic governance.

When engaging stakeholders through a face-to-face process it is important to recruit a manageable number of participants (the Payments Roundtable involved about forty). Participants should be drawn from a wide spectrum of backgrounds and sectors, represent a range of viewpoints, and include many who are in a position to change things. They also must be prepared to work with other stakeholders to develop a better understanding of the issue and potential solutions. And the recruitment process needs to be designed to continually broaden engagement beyond this core group to wider circles.

Throughout the process, engagement should be open and transparent so that all stakeholders are aware of the work and face minimal barriers to participation. At present, face-to-face engagement is still the most effective approach. While social media and other communications technologies excel at raising awareness of an issue and canvassing initial opinions, they cannot yet replicate the intense process of two-way dialogue, learning, and community building we saw in the case of the Payments Roundtable. Over time, as the technology and our understanding of how to use it improves, it should be possible to include many more stakeholders and citizens in the dialogue.[5]

It is helpful to interview participants individually at the outset, especially when face-to-face dialogue is being used. These interviews serve to map participants' views on the issue, how they understand the questions to be addressed, how they see the agenda, and the language they use. This provides valuable insights and gives participants clear evidence that they are being listened to. In addition, feeding back interview results to the full group (without attribution) helps "jump-start" the process.

Once the stakeholders are engaged and the ground rules are understood, participants need to work together to confirm and further develop the initial framing of the issue. This recognizes that when it comes to "wicked problems," the definition of the issue is often unclear and contested. It is important to find common ground on the problem definition at the outset if the dialogue is to be effective.

Step 3: Explore Alternative Perspectives/Futures

The third step in the process is to explore in detail a variety of perspectives on the issue and alternative possibilities for how it may unfold in the future. This provides a way for participants to understand and learn from others' perspectives, and to start to see the limitations of their own.[6] Ensuring that multiple viewpoints are taken into account creates a richer view of the issue and its possibilities. As we have seen, scenario planning offers a powerful and tested methodology for doing this.

Focusing on alternative futures takes the spotlight away from current controversies and creates more opportunities to find common ground; many people find it easier to discover areas of agreement when talking about what they want to see in the future. This focus on the future also places the rationale for change in a broader context: "We need to change because the world has changed."

From the beginning it is important to challenge stakeholders' assumptions and ingrained thinking – for example, through presentations by outside experts. Familiar assumptions often act as blinders, providing a false sense of security and making it more difficult to perceive changes. Successfully challenging those assumptions, as in the case of the Payments Task Force, can open up and energize the learning process.

As we have seen, a dialogue-based process of learning and exploring alternative perspectives and futures can build a community and develop shared mental maps, language, norms, and expectations for that community. Scenarios are an especially effective means of doing this. Scenarios also offer an opportunity to widen the dialogue and expand the community, as when the Payments

Task Force invited additional stakeholders to vet and improve the Roundtable scenarios at the third workshop.

Through this process of learning and exploration, participants come to recognize that the status quo is not likely to persist and that a number of alternative futures are plausible – some attractive and others less so. This awareness lays the groundwork for participants to define and work to realize a more desired future.

Step 4: Co-create the Desired Future

The fourth step in the catalytic governance process is for those stakeholders who are willing (like the Payments Roundtable's "coalition of the willing") to define their more desired future along with practical action steps to realize that future.

To be effective, such a coalition needs to include stakeholders who are in a position to bring about change and willing to take concrete action. Like the working groups that arose out of the Roundtable, these coalitions must first identify those initiatives that will have the largest impact on the future, and then work to make change happen.

Often this will require a process of action learning – taking experimental actions and learning from the result. We can no longer separate planning and action in the traditional way. Instead, in the words of one of the earliest analysts of this world of rapid change, "We must act before we know in order to learn."[7]

Governments or boards (or others responsible for policy) have an important role to play at this stage. First, they need to participate in the dialogue to the degree possible, or at least monitor it closely enough to quickly understand the outcome, anticipate problems, and respond promptly. Without that participation, important initiatives can lose momentum or be stalled altogether (as we saw in the case of the Payments Task Force). Just as important, governments or boards can encourage stakeholders to work together and find common ground by stating early on that they will act on any approach agreed by the participants, provided it meets certain conditions. But they will develop their own solution if participants cannot reach agreement.[8]

Step 5: Ratify and Disseminate the Desired Future

In this fifth step, governments, boards, or others responsible for policy play a leading role, first by ratifying and disseminating the results of the catalytic governance process, and then by acting and encouraging action on the emerging strategy (including legislating if necessary), and monitoring the results. This step is not a simple, once-and-for-all end point; it is itself a process of action learning.

Governments or boards retain the authority not to ratify and even to veto the outcome; however, given the degree of stakeholder engagement and investment in the process to this point, any such veto requires a clear explanation and rationale. Once an outcome is ratified, governments or boards have a responsibility to build widespread support for action, support that goes beyond the stakeholders who have been directly involved in the process. Governments and boards have always had this responsibility, but now they should be able to count on the active support of a cadre of engaged stakeholders.

The government, the private sector, and the social sector need to work together to create and test the new institutions, roles, and practices required to realize the desired future, as well as make the changes necessary to move towards the desired future within their own organizations.

When more is needed (e.g., when the basic framing of the issue is overtaken by events), governments or boards can also use the results as a starting point for reassessing the issue and for a new catalytic governance cycle (of problem framing, engagement and dialogue, exploring alternative perspectives/futures, co-creating a desired future, and acting/encouraging action to realize the desired future).[9]

In most cases it will not be necessary to repeat the full catalytic governance process; instead, simpler variants can be used that build on the work already done. For example, the final published version of the Canadian Payments System Scenarios concluded with a section on how they could be applied and updated, and several organizations used that to test and further develop their own strategies.[10] Another variant is to focus on updating the desired future and the actions needed to realize that future.

Governments, boards, or others responsible for policy need to continuously scan the environment, looking for anomalies that signal important changes that will require a new catalytic governance process or a simpler variant to be initiated. This reassessment can occur months or even years later; a real learning process remains open.

Comparing *Catalytic Governance* to Other Emerging Approaches

A number of approaches to leadership and governance have emerged in recent years as responses to the realities of the information age. While catalytic governance resembles these in some ways, there are also important differences.

Catalytic governance resembles the *catalytic leadership*[11] and *collaborative governance*[12] approaches. All emphasize the interconnectedness of issues and the need to engage a wide range of stakeholders. However, catalytic governance focuses more on the importance of mental maps and on the critical challenge of creating among stakeholders shared frameworks and a shared vision and language, which then provide a basis for collaborative action.

It also resembles *open government*, which along with the concept of *reinventing government* has become prominent in recent years.[13] But while these approaches focus on government, our process centres on *governance*, recognizing that in the information age many more players – including voluntary organizations, the private sector, the media, and more – are deeply involved in the governance process. Catalytic governance also places less emphasis on the release of government information as a primary objective. Providing better access to such information is only one starting point. A more important objective is translating data and information from many sources into useful knowledge. Creating viable knowledge and sustainable solutions requires a broad-based process of engagement, dialogue, and learning in which many can participate, a process that goes well beyond the crowd-sourcing approach that has become a staple of the open government approach.

As we saw in the work of the Payments Task Force, the catalytic governance approach provides rich opportunities for participants to learn from one another, frame and reframe issues, and construct shared mental maps and a common vision that provide a solid basis for collaborative action. These shared mental maps enable people to communicate and work together across boundaries and to organize and govern themselves.

Catalytic governance also shares some similarities with the *open-source governance* approach,[14] which uses lessons from the open source software movement as a model for reforming not only governance but also politics, journalism, and much else. This model has its drawbacks – not least that governance is far more complex than software development (in the memorable words of one analyst: "Should governments really be run like Wikipedia?").[15] More important, in some versions of open source governance, policymakers and political leaders largely disappear; these players remain central to the catalytic governance model, although their role differs from the traditional command-and-control approach.

That different role was well described by Harlan Cleveland when he suggested that in the information society policymakers should be thought of as policy announcers. These leaders, he said, "have the function of passing information back and forth, and in so doing let the consensus amongst the people develop. The bright political leader will then sniff out that consensus and announce it. Others may say that he had made policy. Really what he has done is to enunciate the consensus that had formed."[16]

Catalytic governance emphasizes the importance of having governments, boards, and other governing bodies frame the problem at the outset. At the same time, it also broadens the frame beyond these players' necessarily limited perspective. The involvement of multiple stakeholders necessarily introduces multiple – and sometimes conflicting – views of the problem. Catalytic governance uses the power of dialogue to leverage those multiple perspectives, allowing different viewpoints to emerge, encouraging learning, and frequently leading to a new framing of the problem and new ways forward.

This model also recognizes that policy ends and means cannot be evaluated separately. A wide discussion of both ends and means is necessary for the construction of alternative plausible futures and to lay the basis for inclusive and broad-based action.

Above all, this model emphasizes that fully understanding the policy problem, assessing options for addressing it, and building support for action require public discourse rather than technical expertise alone – serious and open public engagement is indispensable.

Applying and Further Developing Catalytic Governance

Catalytic governance encourages and enables people from diverse backgrounds and interests to work through issues (especially wicked problems); find common ground; construct shared mental maps, norms, and expectations; and begin to act or experiment on that basis. Some examples of when catalytic governance is most needed are listed in box 6.1.

Box 6.1: When to Use Catalytic Governance

Catalytic governance is most needed when simpler, more traditional approaches don't work – for example, when you need to:

- find common ground among multiple stakeholders who have very different problem definitions, perspectives, interests, or mindsets;
- create ownership of a shared vision;
- build trust or credibility with stakeholders;
- address issues where there is no clear definition of the problem (or the definition is contested) and where a purely scientific-rational approach cannot be applied;
- develop breakthrough solutions that can work effectively across boundaries and jurisdictions.

Such challenges, and the wicked problems that create them, are increasingly common in the information age: consider climate change, health care, terrorism, inequality, and many business strategy issues.[17]

If you are a leader facing such an issue, and wish to use a catalytic approach to address it, the next step is to determine how best to engage key stakeholders. As we saw in the case of the Payments System Review, a good way to do this is by mandating a process that will operate at arm's length through a commission or task force.

More traditional task forces and commissions have long been a feature of governance,[18] as a means to draw attention to an issue or to help frame an agenda (or sometimes to delay action on an issue while appearing to act). Catalytic governance and the example of the Payments Task Force offers an updated model of the role a task force or commission needs to play in the information age. Going beyond studying an issue and making recommendations, catalytic governance uses dialogue to actively engage a wider range of stakeholders and catalyse action.

A distinctive feature of issues in the information age is the number and diversity of stakeholders who need (and demand) to be engaged, so that a key governance challenge in all sectors is how to steer effectively when so many hands (with so many different agendas) are on the wheel. Catalytic governance provides a response to that challenge.

An important next step in developing catalytic governance will be to learn more effective ways to use online technology and social media to include many more stakeholders and the public in the process. Currently, this technology excels at raising awareness, assessing top-of-mind opinion, and bringing together the like-minded. But over time, as the technology and our understanding of how best to use it improve, it should be possible to bring people with very different perspectives, assumptions, and interests together in real dialogue. That is a critical next frontier in developing catalytic governance.

Changing Perspective

More fundamentally, in a world of rapidly increasing change and interconnection, we can no longer think of change as a transition between two stable states. In the past, the relative slowness of change allowed us to maintain the illusion of permanence and stability. Today we need to reverse that perspective and to see stable states (including established institutions, frameworks, norms, and roles) as temporary crystallizations of ongoing change. In many respects this has always been the case, and what is involved is less a shift in fact than it is a shift in perspective. (Think of the ways in which the common law has evolved and been reinterpreted to fit changing circumstances.)

Seeing change, rather than stability, as the fundamental context for leadership and governance involves a dramatic shift in perspective – what psychologists refer to as a "figure-ground" shift. It is a bit like the change that occurred in geology with the introduction of plate tectonics – the realization that the apparently solid and enduring geology of the Earth consists of thin plates floating on molten seas.

This new perspective on leadership and governance further underlines why adopting a catalytic approach is so essential in the information age. In the face of rapid change, an information-rich polity, multiplying stakeholders, and fragmenting authority, more traditional top-down approaches do not work and lose their legitimacy. Instead what is needed is to develop a shared sense of direction, a shared mental map and vision among key stakeholders, on the basis of which they can act and coordinate their actions.

As we saw in the case of the Payments Task Force there is an understandable tendency for those in positions of power (e.g., government and the banks) to want to "stay in control." Yet "staying in control" means trying to move into the collaborative and decentralized information age with a hierarchical industrial-age model of decision making. This approach – even working at its peak efficiency – simply cannot address the "wicked problems" and governance challenges of the information age.

In this process the core roles of governments and boards remain as important as ever – in particular, the responsibility to define and protect the broader public interest, including that of the voiceless (in the case of governments), or to ensure that actions are taken in the best interests of the corporation (in the case of boards). In both cases there is a longer-term responsibility of stewardship, including a responsibility to future generations. That public interest or corporate interest cannot be reduced to the sum of stakeholder interests. What does change is not these fundamental responsibilities of governments or boards, but how governments and boards can discharge them effectively in the information age, in particular when transformative change is required.

In this world of rapid change, the solution to any issue or problem is likely to be temporary. What lasts is the continuing process of dialogue and learning that allows people to come together and address those problems.

The experience of the Payments Task Force and subsequent events provide real reason for hope. In addition to the specific steps taken and described earlier, we now understand a great deal more about what is happening in the payments industry and how events are likely to unfold. Those who have participated in the process have developed new mental maps that will allow them to recognize patterns and respond more effectively in this turbulent time – and continue to catalyse their organizations and lead change.

The Payments Task Force did achieve a great deal, and its work will continue to reverberate in the years to come. Above all, it has enabled us to explore and to map a more effective way of governing in the information age – through catalytic governance.

Catalytic governance will continue to evolve as we apply it to different issues in different circumstances and learn from that experience, and as others continue to develop comparable ways to transform leadership and governance for the information age. The version described in this book represents one moment – a snapshot – of that evolution.

We see the publication of this book as a contribution to a growing global dialogue about transforming leadership and governance in the information age. A society or organization's ability to prosper in this world of rapid change will depend, in no small measure, on its ability to develop these new leadership and governance capacities. If you are facing the kinds of challenges listed earlier, where more traditional approaches don't work, we invite you to join this dialogue[19] and to consider what you can do to catalyse action.

Appendix:
Summary of the Scenarios[1]

Scenarios are not predictions and they are not preferences. They are alternative plausible futures, each based on different assumptions. Because scenarios use multiple perspectives to explore problems, rather than just extended and deeper analysis of a single viewpoint, they can help reveal the significance of issues and events that otherwise might be dismissed as unimportant or overlooked altogether.

The scenarios developed by the Payments Roundtable aimed to stretch thinking about both opportunities and obstacles that the future might hold. As a whole, the scenario set captures a range of possibilities, good and bad, expected and surprising.

The four scenarios were primarily defined and differentiated by a set of key uncertainties: eventualities that will turn out one way in one scenario, and a different way in another. The Payments Roundtable identified many potential uncertainties and ultimately selected what its members saw as the two most significant critical uncertainties that would shape the future of the CPS:

- How well aligned is the CPS ecosystem?
- How rapid is consumer and user adoption?

These two branching points – the degree of alignment of the CPS ecosystem (aligned or fragmented) and the extent of consumer adoption (rapid or moderate) – were used to create a set of four future scenarios for the CPS that are divergent, challenging, internally consistent, and plausible (see figure 7.1).

Figure 7.1: Canadian Payments System Scenarios: Branching Points

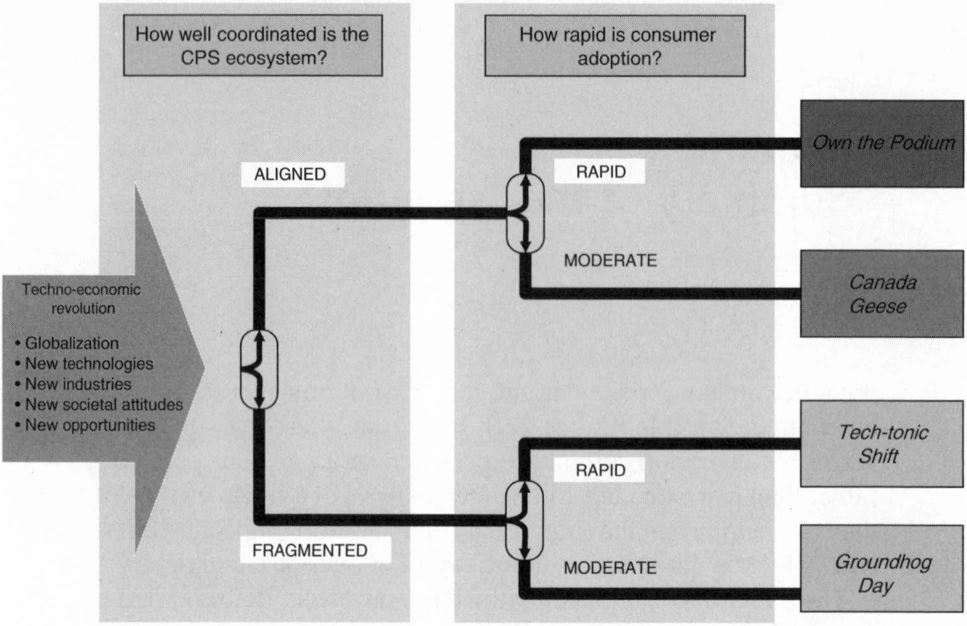

Groundhog Day – Fragmented Ecosystem and Moderate Consumer Adoption

Like the movie *Groundhog Day*, this scenario replays the recent past. Canada's payments system moves forward as it has in the past. Not much changes in the infrastructure of the payments system. The ecosystem is not strongly aligned: government, financial institutions (FIs), businesses, and telecommunications companies (telcos) are all charting their own courses and protecting their own interests, with few or no universal standards.

The regulatory environment responds slowly and as a rule offers only basic protection, except when specific crises force a more significant response. At the same time, consumers and businesses are slow to adopt new technology; mobile payments move slowly; concerns about authentication, privacy, and security remain high; and no clear product winners drive consumers to embrace a new technology strongly. Meanwhile, much of the rest of the world moves ahead, adopting new technologies and creating a more robust regulatory framework.

Tech-tonic Shift – Fragmented Ecosystem and Rapid Consumer Adoption

Technology companies such as Google, Apple, and social networking sites develop alternative payments platforms and become major players. Government is slow to regulate, and competition is fierce. Several factors aid the success of these companies, including high consumer adoption and cheap new technological platforms. New entrants take advantage of cloud computing and collaborative networks to create low-cost scalable businesses. The proliferation of new financial services and applications to address specific needs is phenomenal.

The first half of the decade sees increasing fragmentation in the marketplace, with a wide range of different user systems, each with different interfaces and authentication methods. The traditional financial institutions (FIs) find themselves under great pressure. Although consumers and businesses benefit from convenient new products, at the same time fraud rises and security breaches become more widespread, as do legal cases involving liability. Responding to growing pressure from businesses and consumers, and following a major security breach at an alternative FI, the government moves to regulate the new entrants more actively. In the latter part of the decade, alternative FIs come to terms with new government regulation, and there is consolidation in this market. Many consumers and businesses enjoy the new and convenient payment options, but some are left behind. In the space of a decade, innovative new technologies and market forces have fuelled a tectonic shift in the way Canadians transact.

Canada Geese – Aligned Ecosystem and Moderate Consumer Adoption

Like a flock of Canada geese, the payments system is strongly aligned and cooperative. All parties – federal and provincial governments, FIs, telcos, networks, merchants, and other players – operate on a level playing field. Over the course of the decade, this high level of collaboration reduces friction in the system: the framework of the CPS is expanded to include all players who work together to agree on the rules and standards, spurred by the understanding that, if they don't, government will act with a heavier regulatory hand.

Because the system is reasonably efficient and the major players are happy enough, there is limited push towards new technology, and the cost of meeting standards and regulatory requirements slows innovation. Instead, the payments system prioritizes gradual, thoughtful, evidence-based reform that embraces the best of technologies being road-tested in other systems. This allows Canada to benefit from innovations while avoiding the risk and disruption of working on the bleeding edge.

Own the Podium – Aligned Ecosystem and Rapid Consumer Adoption

There is growing awareness of the magnitude and speed of changes being fuelled by the convergence of computing and connectivity into the smart phone, disrupting existing business models and ways of working while creating huge new opportunities. Nowhere are both the threat and the opportunity clearer than in Canada's payments system. Responding to this challenge, industry comes together to facilitate the rapid development of a set of standards in key areas of payment – especially privacy, security, digital identification and authentication, and mobile payments – that will encourage competition and innovation and allow Canada to lead developments elsewhere in the world. This effort is reminiscent of the "Own the Podium" campaign at the 2010 Olympics, when Canada moved away from traditional approaches to win the most gold medals ever for a Winter Olympics host country.

Canada sees remarkable shifts to new ways of processing payments and other transactions. The principle that Canadians "own their own data" and the accompanying robust digital identification and authentication systems that are developed are crucial in encouraging rapid consumer adoption and allowing Canada to capitalize on the massive changes under way. Companies use cloud computing and collaborative networks to set up payments businesses quickly in response to consumer needs. Lessons learned in payments quickly flow to other sectors, such as health. In financial institutions and other industries there is much disruption and considerable job loss but also the creation of new industries and new jobs. By 2020 Canada is a global leader in this new online world, and is exporting its expertise and systems to the global community.

Notes

Introduction: Leadership and Governance in the Information Age

1 The interplay of social and technological dynamics that defines the information age is discussed in chapter 1.

2 For example, in their ground-breaking book *Why Nations Fail* (New York: Crown, 2012), Daron Acemoglu and James Robinson convincingly show that man-made political and economic institutions underlie economic success (or lack of it). They argue that inclusive political institutions in support of inclusive economic institutions are the key to sustained prosperity. Institutions, leadership, and governance processes designed for the "command and control" industrial age must be replaced with "conferring and networking" in the information age in order to get things done.

3 For additional detail, see Steven A. Rosell, *Renewing Governance: Governing by Learning in the Information Age* (Oxford and New York: Oxford University Press, 1999).

4 In society and politics, a catalytic process is one that provokes or speeds significant change or action, or that precipitates an event. Transformative change is profound, fundamental, and irreversible. It is a radical shift in thinking, assumptions, perception, and viewpoint – change that precludes a return to previous mental maps and that leads to large alterations in external behaviour.

5 A good review of this literature and presentation of the new focus can be found in S.A. Haslam, S.D. Reicher, and M.J. Platow, *The New Psychology of Leadership: Identity, Authority and Power* (New York: Psychology Press, 2011). A valuable precursor is W.H. Drath and C.J. Palus, *Making Common Sense: Leadership as Meaning-making in a Community of Practice* (Greensboro, NC: Center for Creative Leadership, 1994).

6 Harlan Cleveland, "The Twilight of Hierarchy: Speculations on the Global Information Society," *Public Administration Review,* 45 (1) (Jan.–Feb. 1985): 185–95.

7 The groundbreaking statement on wicked problems is H. Rittel and M. Webber, "Dilemmas in a General Theory of Planning," *Policy Sciences,* 4(1973): 155–69. According to Rittel and Webber, wicked problems have the following ten characteristics:

1. **Wicked problems have no definitive formulation.**
2. **Wicked problems have no stopping rule**: since you can't define the problem in any single way, it's difficult to tell when it's resolved.
3. **Solutions to wicked problems are not true or false, but good or bad:** the best to be hoped for is a solution that is "good enough."
4. **There is no immediate or ultimate test of a solution to a wicked problem:** the only way to test a solution is to put it in place.
5. **Every implemented solution to a wicked problem has consequences**, and it's impossible to know in advance how these will play out.
6. **Wicked problems don't have a well-described set of potential solutions**.
7. **Each wicked problem is essentially unique.**
8. **Each wicked problem can be considered a symptom of another problem** – and each proposed resolution will generate its own set of unique problems.
9. **The causes of a wicked problem can be explained in numerous ways,** and different stakeholders will have different but equally valid explanations.
10. **The planner (designer) has no right to be wrong:** she will be held liable for the consequences of whatever action is instigated.

8 For these and other examples see Australian Public Services Commission, *Tackling Wicked Problems* (Canberra: Author, 2007); and John C. Camillus, "Strategy as a Wicked Problem," *Harvard Business Review* 86 (May 2008): 98–101. A good recent discussion of the challenges posed by wicked problems and of the importance of broader public engagement in addressing those challenges is in Daniel Yankelovich's *Wicked Problems, Workable Solutions: Lessons from a Public Life* (Lanham, MD: Rowman and Littlefield, 2014).

9 The task force members were: Brad Badeau, an accountant and entrepreneur with financial services industry experience from Ontario; Stephane Le Bouyonnec, an engineer with a technology and private equity investment background from Quebec; John Chant, an economics professor

emeritus from British Columbia; Laura Gillham, a marketing and branding executive from the Maritimes; Lili de Grandpré, a former corporate bank executive and strategy consultant from Quebec; Pat Meredith, a former senior bank executive and strategy consultant from Toronto and northern Ontario; and Terry Wright, a lawyer and former chief legal counsel for a financial holding company in Manitoba. In addition to representing a wide range of relevant expertise and geographic and gender diversity, the task force members also represented a range of ages, from mid-thirties to late-seventies.

1 The Global Information Society

1 At the same time, more people are *inadequately* educated. The widening divide between those who have the skills and education to thrive in an information economy and those who do not is an increasingly pressing issue in the information society.
2 Somewhat paradoxically, the increase of information availability can lead to greater confusion and disagreement, as different interpretations and data sets vie with one another. This point is elaborated in D.N. Michael, "Governing by Learning in an Information Society," in Steven A. Rosell, *Governing in an Information Society* (Ottawa: Institute for Research on Public Policy, 1992), 121–33.
3 For example, as globalization makes nation-state boundaries less salient, we see populations around the world trying to reorganize themselves around more conspicuous economic or ethnic boundaries (for example, Scotland and South Sudan). Globalization and regional fragmentation can be seen as parts of the same process of restructuring.
4 The disclosures of Edward Snowden and WikiLeaks are only some of the most dramatic recent examples.
5 Harlan Cleveland, "The Twilight of Hierarchy: Speculations on the Global Information Society," *Public Administration Review,* 45 (1) (Jan.–Feb. 1984): 185–95.
6 The blossoming of the information economy also can be seen as arising from the burgeoning demand for better ways to interpret: to translate data and information into knowledge.
7 Carlota Perez, *Technological Revolutions and Financial Capital: The Dynamics of Bubbles and Golden Ages* (London, Elgar, 2002; available at: http://www.carlotaperez.org/pubs) also includes a more recent wave starting in the twenty-first century: that of biotech, nanotech, bioelectronics, and new materials.
8 Cleveland, "The Twilight of Hierarchy."

9 Source: Internet Live Stats at: www.Internetlivestats.com/internet-users.
10 Source: eMarketer at http://www.emarketer.com/Article/
Smartphone-Users-Worldwide-Will-Total-175-Billion-2014/1010536.
11 Drastic innovations (also known as "general purpose technologies"
[GPTs]) are those that can be used in a wide range of sectors in ways that
drastically change the way those sectors, the economy, and society operate. GPTs are characterized by the following features:

1. They are extremely pervasive; that is, they are used as inputs by a
   wide range of sectors in the economy.
2. They have the potential for technical advances, which manifests itself
   in sustained improvements in performance.
3. Complementarities with their user sectors arise in manufacturing or in
   the R&D technology.

These features allow GPTs to act as "engines of growth." Each
improvement in a GPT leads to its adoption by an increasing number of user sectors and fosters complementary advances that make
its adoption even more attractive. Both these factors drive increased
demand for the GPT, which in turn spurs further technical progress
in the GPT, leading to a new round of advances downstream, and so
forth. As the use of a GPT spreads throughout the economy, its effects
become significant at the aggregate level, thus affecting overall growth.
The history of technology suggests that changes in technology and
changes in organization and institutions are intimately related, and
that tangible investments in the latter as GPTs open up new opportunities may be critical for growth. These points are articulated in *General
Purpose Technologies and Economic Growth*, edited by Elhanan Helpman
(Cambridge: MIT Press, 1998).
12 As of June 2014 the Google Play Store and the Apple App Store each
hold 1.2 million applications for download. Within the Google Play Store
consumers have downloaded apps a total of roughly *80 billion times.*
Likewise, on 2 June 2014, *TechCrunch* reported that there had been 75
billion Apple App Store downloads to date: http://www.informit.com/
blogs/blog.aspx?uk=The-Fight-for-The-Mobile-App-Market-Android-
vs-iOS.
13 A recent McKinsey study examined the probable growth of global
flows over the next twenty years. It found potential for dramatic
expansion in the scope and complexity of cross-border exchanges.
Two major forces are driving this expansion: increasing global

prosperity and the growing pervasiveness of Internet connectivity and digital technologies. See McKinsey Global Institute, *Global Flows in a Digital Age: How Trade, Finance, People and Data Connect the World Economy*, April 2014. Available at: http://www.mckinsey.com/ MGI_Globalflows_Full_report_April2014.

14 The following are significant milestones in the history of the CPS (2000–10):

1. Due to the success of Interac, by 2003 *Canadians became the highest per-capita users of debit cards* in the world.
2. Adoption of *chip and PIN* (Personal Identification Number) *technology* was mandated in response to an increase in debit and credit card fraud. Chip and PIN roll-out began in 2008.
3. In fall 2008, MasterCard and Visa released *contactless cards* to capture a larger segment of small cash payments.
4. Recognizing the growing popularity of alternative payment methods, in 2009 major wireless carriers in Canada formed a strategic partnership to develop Zoompass, Canada's first major *mobile phone payment service*.
5. In 2010 the minister of finance created the Debit and Credit Card Code of Conduct to protect merchant and consumer interests.

15 The clearing and settlement of small payments in Canada still occurs in batches through the Automated Clearing and Settlement System (ACSS) in the middle of the night, without finality of payment for two to three days. At least seven countries – China, the Czech Republic, Mexico, Switzerland, South Africa, and Singapore – have implemented Immediate Funds Transfer Systems that allow clearing and settlement to take place immediately.

16 The U.K. Payments Council attempted to mandate the end of cheques by 2018, but was forced to rescind its decision. Despite this, cheque usage for B2B payments in the United Kingdom, northern Europe, and Australia is already below 10 per cent.

17 Digital technology is changing not only how we pay but also what we pay. New currencies, such as Bitcoins and others, bypass traditional bank clearing and settlement, reducing barriers and costs.

18 Cleveland, "The Twilight of Hierarchy," 185–6. Emphasis added.

2 Engagement and Dialogue

1 Research papers can be obtained through the Payments Task Force website: http://paymentsystemreview.ca/index.php/home/index.html.

2 The members of the Payments Roundtable are listed at the beginning of the book (see pages xvii–xviii).

3 EMV stands for Europay, MasterCard, and Visa, a global standard for inter-operation of integrated circuit cards (IC cards or "chip cards") and IC card capable point of sale (POS) terminals and automated teller machines (ATMs), for authenticating credit and debit card transactions.

4 See http://www.viewpointlearning.com, which also includes reports and articles on many of these projects.

5 This chart is designed to emphasize the differences between debate and dialogue, not to elaborate the many positive aspects of debate. The charts in the rest of this chapter were prepared by Viewpoint Learning and used to brief the Roundtable on using dialogue at its first meeting. For additional background, see Daniel Yankelovich, *The Magic of Dialogue* (New York: Simon and Schuster, 2001).

6 More on the process can be found at Royal Dutch Shell, "Exploring the Future," 2001. (See: http://www.shell.com/global/future-energy/scenarios/explorers-guide.html.) See also Steven A. Rosell, *Renewing Governance* (Oxford and New York: Oxford University Press, 1999).

7 All summaries and meeting reports included extensive quotations from Roundtable participants, but these comments were presented without attribution.

8 See, for example, Steven A. Rosell, "A Missing Step in the Governance Process," *Development*, 47(4) (2004): 43–9; and G.R. Davis, *Scenarios as a Tool for the 21st Century*, Probing the Future Conference, Strathclyde University, July 2002.

3 Exploring Perspectives and Building Scenarios

1 Royal Dutch Shell, "People and Connections, Global Scenarios to 2020," 2001 (see: https://www.pik-potsdam.de/avec/peyresq2005/talks/0921/leemans/literature/shell_global_scenarios.pdf); and Earth Resources Development Council, State of Victoria, Australia, "Victorian Brown Coal in a Carbon Constrained World," January 2010 (see: http://www.energyandresources.vic.gov.au/earth-resources/victorias-earth-resources/coal/scenario-development-program-report).

2 World Business Council for Sustainable Development, "Exploring Sustainable Development," November 1998 (see: http://www.wbcsd.org/Pages/EDocument/EDocumentDetails.aspx?ID=143&NoSearchContextKey=true); and Intergovernmental Panel on Climate Change, "Special Report on Emissions Scenarios," 2001 (see: https://www.ipcc.ch/pdf/special-reports/spm/sres-en.pdf).

3 UNAIDS, "AIDS in Africa: Three Scenarios to 2025," January 2005
   (see: http://data.unaids.org/publications/IRC-pub07/jc1058-
   aidsinafrica_en.pdf).
4 See the discussion of mental maps in chapter 2.
5 For those interested in the broader application of collaborative scenario
   building in society, see: G.R. Davis, *Scenarios as a Tool for the 21st Century*,
   Probing the Future Conference, Strathclyde University, July 2002; and
   G.R. Davis, *Exploring Societal Problems*, World Conservation Union
   (IUCN) Futures Dialogues, International Union for Conservation of
   Nature Environment Centre, Johannesburg, August 2002.
6 John Seely Brown is Co-chair of the Deloitte Center for the Edge and a
   visiting scholar and adviser to the provost at the University of Southern
   California (USC). Prior to that he was the chief scientist of Xerox
   Corporation and the director of its Palo Alto Research Center (PARC).
7 John Seely Brown's presentation is available at http://www.catalytic
   governance.com/the-future-of-the-canadian-payments-system/#jsb.
8 The SixthSense prototype consists of a tiny wearable projector and
   camera connected to a mobile computing device that can be carried in
   the user's pocket. The device projects visual information onto nearby
   surfaces, walls, and physical objects – turning them into interfaces. At
   the same time the camera recognizes and tracks the user's hand gestures
   and physical objects: the user can do many of the things now possible
   with a phone or tablet, but with no need for a handheld device – the surrounding environment acts as the touchscreen and interface.
9 See http://www.pranavmistry.com/projects/sixthsense/.
   Pranav Mistry's talk was based on his remarkable TED talk in
   November 2009 which is available at: http://www.ted.com/talks/
   pranav_mistry_the_thrilling_potential_of_sixthsense_technology.
10 This presentation is available at: http://www.catalyticgovernance.com/
   the-future-of-the-canadian-payments-system/#kristpherhaag.
11 This belief stemmed from the fact that Canada was a leader in the use
   of credit and debit cards for retail purchases.
12 Participants wrestled with the question of what the most appropriate timeframe should be. The pace of technological change led some
   participants to suggest a five-year horizon. Others maintained that the
   practicalities of changing the framework governing payments made a
   ten- to fifteen-year timeframe more realistic. After some dialogue, the
   Roundtable ultimately agreed on a ten-year timeframe, recognizing that
   this horizon could be adjusted if needed.
13 Source: Annual Fraud Report (2009), CyberSource Corporation.
14 Source: Kaspersky Lab.

15 These presentations can be found at: http://www.catalyticgovernance
    .com/the-future-of-the-canadian-payments-system/#gregwolfond;
    http://www.catalyticgovernance.com/the-future-of-the-canadian-
    payments-system/#andrewnash; and http://www.catalyticgovernance
    .com/the-future-of-the-canadian-payments-system/#peterwatkins.
16 These presentations can be found at: http://www.catalyticgovernance
    .com/the-future-of-the-canadian-payments-system/#vincedagostino;
    http://www.catalyticgovernance.com/the-future-of-the-canadian-
    payments-system/#andrewdresner; and http://www.catalyticgovernance
    .com/the-future-of-the-canadian-payments-system/#michaelmcderment.
17 One unobtrusive measure of the degree to which Canada was lagging
    in B2B was how difficult it was to find Canadian expert presenters with
    in-depth knowledge of new products and services in the B2B space.
18 These presentations can be found at: http://www.catalyticgovernance.
    com/the-future-of-the-canadian-payments-system/#mickeymcmanus;
    http://www.catalyticgovernance.com/the-future-of-the-canadian-
    payments-system/#michaeladams; and http://www.catalytic
    governance.com/the-future-of-the-canadian-payments-system/
    #juliettepowell.
19 There are three basic approaches to building scenarios:

    • *Normative:* This approach begins by describing a desired future, and
      works backwards from there to understand whether that future is
      plausible and what it would take to get there.
    • *Deductive:* This approach identifies the most important uncertainties
      about the future, and then uses these uncertainties as axes defining
      a grid or matrix. Each quadrant on the matrix describes a different
      possible way the key uncertainties might play out – a scenario. The
      development of each scenario outlines the story of how we might get
      to that particular future, the key events, and what it would look like
      when we arrive.
    • *Inductive:* This approach reverses the *deductive* approach. Rather than
      starting with the key uncertainties about the future and construct-
      ing scenarios based on different ways those uncertainties might play
      out, the inductive approach starts with possible futures and works
      backwards to determine what the framing uncertainties must be.
      The process starts by looking at what would happen if specific chains
      of events were to take place and constructing a plausible storyline
      for each chain. After developing several such storylines, participants
      then need to identify the critical uncertainties at issue and develop

the scenario structure. Whichever approach is taken, the scenarios do not evolve in an organized, linear fashion. Generally the starting point is a short narrative and a number of likely future events. These are developed into a full-fledged storyline, supported by sound research, quantification, and modelling. The storylines often change significantly in the process, as it becomes clear that some elements are inconsistent or irrelevant, and as research and quantification open up new insights. The result is an iterative interplay of narrative, research, and quantification.

20 These presentations can be found at: http://www.catalyticgovernance. com/the-future-of-the-canadian-payments-system/#davidbirch; http:// www.catalyticgovernance.com/the-future-of-the-canadian-payments-system/#chrishamilton; and http://www.catalyticgovernance.com/ the-future-of-the-canadian-payments-system/#stevemott.

21 Post-Carousel Feedback: Top Questions and Priorities for Improving the Four Scenarios:

Groundhog Day
- Need to acknowledge the risks posed by the outside world changing around us and how this will impact Canada and Canadians.
- Need to consider how much advances in mobile technology will impact the industry over the next 10–12 years.
- Merchants not likely to want to make changes in their infrastructure to accommodate Visa and MasterCard.
- Scenario seems too slow – many of these changes are already taking place: e.g., EFT increasing, use of cheques decreasing, use of EDI increasing.
- Need more discussion of fixes required in ID and fraud – having fraud grow out of control is not acceptable.
- Are the timelines feasible, especially with respect to B2B?
- Will government really be so standoffish? Is this realistic?
- Segmentation: different sectors have different interests. Can scenario reflect this better?

Tech-tonic Shift
- Need to focus more on B2B – too retail-focused as written.
- Can you have mass adoption in a fragmented environment?
- Too much emphasis on global players and not enough on what happens to existing Canadian players/infrastructure.

- How many networks and different payment terminals are there – 5? 15? 50?
- If there are clusters of technological forward thinkers, it seems unlikely that a security breach would affect all of them. It's more likely that one would be affected and the others move in to grab market share.
- Rapid adoption: is it culturally un-Canadian? Consortium creation within 18 months is unlikely.
- The overall costs are not taken into account, and the business case is largely glossed over.
- A single massive security breach is unlikely; it's more likely to be several small breaches that lead to changes in regulation.

Canada Geese
- "Light" regulation is not plausible – natural market forces won't permit this kind of scenario. Instead, more governance will be required, and it will need teeth.
- Need more attention to privacy and security.
- Globalization is not well covered – too Canada-centric.
- Be more generic with respect to the "revised CPA." Call it something else, and focus on what it will do.
- Can these groups happily collaborate?
- Need to focus not just on product features but also on industry concerns – how can we move away from industry utility model?

Internet Inukshuk
- Is this too optimistic? Collaboration requires organizations to want to collaborate. Some players don't feel this – does Apple really feel the need to collaborate?
- Government limitations seem to be implausible.
- Need better understanding of the costs and benefits of new technology.
- Eliminating cheques altogether is not realistic – "reduction" is more plausible given the demographic factors at work.
- It may be risky for Canada to lead authentication development on our own. If the rest of the world goes elsewhere, what happens to our investment?
- Businesses are going to need time to make changes, at the back end & POS.
- Need to clarify rules for liability.
- Is provincial harmony really likely?

- You can't just say that everyone will participate – you have to set up hard discussions about "who gives what" and "who gets what."

4 Developing a Governance Framework for the Canadian Payments System

1 Under the Canadian constitution, the federal government regulates financial institutions and the provincial governments are responsible for consumer protection. As a result, most payments legislation has focused on financial institutions, yet almost half of payment transactions are provided by non-financial institutions, such as Visa, MasterCard, PayPal, and TransUnion.

2 The task force identified four challenges it believed must be addressed for Canada to become a leader in payments:

1. increasing fairness in credit and debit card networks;
2. updating the regulatory and governance structure;
3. improving online authentication, security, and privacy; and
4. transitioning to a digital economy.

These challenges were described in *The Way We Pay*, chapter 3, pages 12–18.

3 This methodology was developed by Roger Martin and his colleagues at Monitor Group (a strategy consulting firm founded by Michael Porter; now Monitor Deloitte, the strategy service line of Deloitte Consulting). A description of Strategic Choice Structuring was included in *The Responsibility Virus* by Roger Martin, published in 2000, and more recently in *Playing to Win* by A.G. Lafley and Roger Martin, published in 2013. The process was tested at CIBC and P&G in the late 1990s and has been used to successfully develop and implement strategy in many diverse settings since.

4 The task force realized that there was no solution at either end of the continuum – no regulation (the status quo through a voluntary code of conduct) had not resolved the credit/debit card issue; and government regulation, as the Australians had discovered, was too inflexible in a rapidly changing environment.

5 The "law of requisite variety," developed by W.R. Ashby (*Introduction to Cybernetics*, 1956) applies here. The law states that only variety can master variety. In other words, regulation is possible only if the

regulating system is as information rich and flexible as the system to be regulated.

6 The working groups were: Digital ID and Authentication; Electronic Invoicing and Payments; Mobile Payments; Infrastructure; and the SGO Start-up Group. Consumer, governance, and regulatory advisory groups were also created.

7 *The Way We Pay*, pages 23–30. This document was released at the end of June 2011 (later than originally planned) because the government did not want the task force work to be released during the federal election.

5 Co-creating a Desired Future

1 The transition from paper-based to digital payments was already under way elsewhere, although no country was leading in all types of payments (retail, business to business, and government).

2 D.J. Snowden and M.D. Boone, "A Leader's Framework for Decision Making," *Harvard Business Review* (November 2007): 69–76.

3 For a summary see Mike Pedler (ed.), *Action Learning in Practice* (Burlington, VT: Gower Publishing, 2012).

4 See, for example, Kurt Lewin, "Action Research and Minority Problems," *Journal of Social Issues,* 2(4) (1946): 34–46; and D.J. Greenwood and M. Levin, *Introduction to Action Research* (Thousand Oaks, CA: Sage Publications, 2007). Action research techniques were further developed and applied to a range of organizational issues, especially by the Tavistock Institute. Between 1990 and 1997, the University of Pennsylvania Press published a three-volume anthology of this work under the title *The Social Engagement of Social Science*. A variant of this approach, Participatory Action Research (PAR), has been applied, especially in organizational and community development. In PAR the subjects of the research become part of the research team. One good overview of this work is William F. Whyte (ed.), *Participatory Action Research* (Thousand Oaks, CA: Sage Publications, 1991).

5 With the exception of the SGO Working Group, which was chaired by one of the members of the Payments Roundtable, Barbara Stymiest.

6 See http://paymentsystemreview.ca/wp-content/themes/psr-esp-hub/documents/r03_eng.pdf.

7 See http://paymentsystemreview.ca/index.php/papers/policy-papers/index.html.

8 With the help of McKinsey and Company, the task force projected the potential savings of transitioning to digital payments. The $7.7 billion

potential annual savings from implementing electronic invoicing and payments for 80 per cent of B2B transactions represented only a small part of the tremendous opportunity at hand. A thoroughly digital payments system underpinning online delivery of private and public goods and services could save the Canadian economy as much as 2 per cent of GDP in productivity gains, equivalent to $32 billion in annual savings. As important as this massive benefit is the fact that such a Canadian payments system will lead to far greater choice, efficiency, and convenience for consumers, businesses, governments, and organizations, as well as a safer and more secure system.

9 The banks were reluctant to pay a fee to the wireless carriers to load credit cards onto the phone's SIM card. In their view, there was not sufficient demand from customers to justify the additional cost or to support the business case for investment in mobile payments. They were also concerned that this would open the door for wireless carriers to usurp their customer relationship.

10 The working group also recognized the importance of having an "anchor user," such as transit, to support the business case and speed adoption. Unfortunately, transportation providers in Canada are very fragmented and not likely to support a single solution.

11 Task Force for the Payments System Review, *Going Digital*, 43.
  (See http://paymentsystemreview.ca/wp-content/themes/psr-esp-hub/documents/r03_eng.pdf.)

12 According to Interac, 11 per cent of all terminals were NFC enabled in 2011. However, penetration of high-volume terminals such as grocery stores was estimated at close to 50 per cent.

13 At this time, only Blackberry (RIM) and certain Android mobile devices are supported.

14 It is arguable that convenience trumps trust. Consumers, especially millennials, have demonstrated their willingness to access online services without the security and privacy afforded by digital identification and authentication regimes.

15 Much of the technical groundwork for DIA in Canada had been done by the federal government and the province of British Columbia. Late in 2011 the federal government negotiated an umbrella contract with a supplier that could be extended to any province choosing to join the DIA regime.

16 Most (86 per cent) of the population resides in four provinces – Ontario, Quebec, British Columbia, and Alberta. Six banks, two credit union systems, and three wireless carriers supply most financial and communications services.

17 Progress in the working group discussions was achieved by focusing on use cases that allowed participants to see and understand the business opportunity, necessary controls, privacy implications, and possible technology architectures enough to begin to clarify their own business model.

18 As discussed earlier in this chapter, these principles were developed by the Consumer Advisory Group and reviewed by the Regulatory Advisory Group to provide a starting point for the development of principles-based payment oversight in legislation.

19 The Task Force for the Payments System Review report, *Moving Canada into the Digital Age,* was released to the public in March 2012 and can be found at http://paymentsystemreview.ca/index.php/papers/moving-canada-into-the-digital-age/index.html. Recommendations can be found on page 10 of the final report.

20 Canada slid to fourteenth place in 2014 from ninth five years earlier in the World Economic Forum's Competitiveness Ranking. Northern European countries such as Finland, Sweden, the Netherlands, Germany, and the United Kingdom continued to improve their rankings, in part because of increased efficiencies in administration and payments and innovative products and services facilitated by payments infrastructure investments.

21 Since 2012, PWGSC has included letters explaining that the federal government will not send cheques after April 2016 and encouraging citizens to complete enclosed pre-authorized credit enrolment forms with every cheque and statement it mailed to citizens. Canada Revenue Agency has also promoted online bill payment and pre-authorized debits for taxes and other levies, following the closure of most of its physical tax collection offices in 2013.

22 Because Apple is a closed system (it provides both the hardware and software), it ensures that all apps downloaded on its devices comply with its standards. Apple Pay, introduced in September 2014, is discussed later in this chapter.

23 Although Japan has had mobile phone payments for more than a decade, these payments are restricted to small payments from a user's telephone account (not his or her bank account).

24 The key elements of the legislation require the following governance changes:

Changes to the Board of Directors:
- Create a smaller, majority independent board – the size of the board would be reduced from 16 to 13 members, the Bank of Canada would no longer sit on the board, and there would no longer be ministerial appointees.

- Two classes of directors would be elected by all CPA members:
  - » 7 independent directors (eligibility criteria would be determined in forthcoming regulations);
  - » 5 member directors (3 of whom must be direct participants in CPA systems).
- The president of the CPA would become an ex-officio member of the board.
- The chairperson and deputy chair would be selected from among the independent directors.
- A nominating committee would be established to identify qualified candidates to serve as directors.

New Accountability Framework:
- The board would submit a five-year corporate plan annually to the minister of finance for approval.
- The board would publish an annual report, including audited financial statements and a report from the chairperson on the Stakeholder Advisory Counsel.
- The board would have authority for approving the operating and capital budgets of the association.
- The minister of finance's directive power would be expanded to issue directives to the CPA in any instance where the minister deems it to be in the public interest to do so.

Other Changes:
- A new Members Advisory Council would be established, to advise the board on technical and operational aspects associated with the operation of CPA systems and the development of new technologies.
- All votes by CPA members would occur on a one-member, one-vote basis.

25 Initially, Apple will receive 15 to 30 basis points of the approximately 1.5 per cent interchange fee on credit card transactions to compensate it for this security.
26 In March 2015, Samsung, the manufacturer of the world's most popular smartphone, which uses Google's Android operating system, announced the launch of Samsung Pay in the United States and South Korea, followed by Europe and China.
27 For example, Apple – which supports more than half of mobile banking apps in Canada (a good indication of its likely share of mobile payments) – is outside the Canadian Payments Association, proposed legislation, and the voluntary mobile code of conduct.

6 Lessons Learned and the Catalytic Governance Model

1 Final Report, Task Force for the Payments System Review, page 4.
2 Such spaces are often used when working on major change efforts with individuals, groups, or organizations. Examples include *transitional spaces, parallel learning structures,* and *communities of practice.* The Payments Task Force tried to provide something similar at the level of national governance. On transitional space and transitional objects see D.W. Winnicott, *Playing and Reality* (London: Tavistock, 1971); on parallel learning structures see G.R. Bushe and A.B. Shani, *Parallel Learning Structures: Increasing Innovation in Bureaucracies* (Boston: Addison-Wesley, 1990); on communities of practice, see Etienne Wenger, *Communities of Practice: Learning, Meaning, and Identity* (Cambridge: Cambridge University Press, 1998).
3 The philosopher Jürgen Habermas provided a seminal description of three still-predominant models of public decision making. These are the "decisionist," "technocratic," and "pragmatic" models. See Jürgen Habermas, *Toward a Rational Society* (Boston: Beacon Press, 1971). This chapter (and in particular figures 6.1, 6.2, and 6.3) draws upon Ottmar Edenhofer and Martin Kowarsch, "A Pragmatist Concept of Scientific Policy Advice": http://www.mcc-berlin.net/fileadmin/data/pdf/Edenhofer_Kowarsch_PEM_Manuscript_2012.pdf.
4 It is also termed the "democratic," "co-production," "deliberative," or "co-evolutionary" model.
5 For example, in other work we have been experimenting with ways to replicate online the norms of dialogue and the sense of community, mutual respect, and learning from each other that we see in an effective FTF process, in place of the "flame wars" that are all too common on today's Internet. Another possibility is to explore the degree to which observing a dialogue (or dramatizations of a dialogue) that includes some participants with whom they can identify enables viewers to engage in that learning process. Our colleague Daniel Yankelovich, in *The Magic of Dialogue* (New York: Simon & Schuster, 2001), has termed such an approach "proxy dialogue."
6 Those limitations become visible when you see that others who come from a different perspective with different assumptions perceive the same "reality" in radically different ways.
7 Donald Schön, *Beyond the Stable State* (New York: W.W. Norton, 1973).
8 We are grateful for this suggestion to Arthur Kroeger, CC, called the dean of deputy ministers in Canada, who often used this approach in successful multi-stakeholder efforts.

9 This also recognizes that wicked problems have no stopping rule, and that the process does not end until stakeholders lose interest, resources are depleted, or political realities change.

10 See: Viewpoint Learning, in association with the Scenarios Roundtable and the Canadian Task Force for the Payments System Review (2011). *Scenarios for the Future of the Canadian Payments System*: http://paymentsystemreview.ca/wp-content/themes/psr-esp-hub/documents/r01_eng.pdf.

11 Jeffrey S. Luke, *Catalytic Leadership: Strategies for an Interconnected World* (San Francisco: Jossey-Bass, 1998).

12 "Collaborative governance" is a process and a form of governance in which participants (parties, agencies, stakeholders) representing different interests are collectively empowered to make a policy decision or make recommendations to a final decision maker who will not substantially change consensus recommendations from the group. See John D. Donahue and Richard J. Zeckhauser, *Collaborative Governance: Private Roles for Public Goals in Turbulent Times* (Princeton, NJ: Princeton University Press, 2011).

13 "Open government" is the governing doctrine holding that citizens have a right of access to the documents and proceedings of the government to allow for effective public oversight. In its broadest construction it opposes reason of state and other considerations, which have tended to legitimize extensive state secrecy. For more on open government see, for example "Canada's Action Plan on Open Government," Government of Canada, 18 March 2011; Peter S. Orszag, "Open Government Directive (USA)," United States Government, 8 December 2009; and the website of the Open Government Partnership at http://www.opengovpartnership.org. See also David Osborne and Ted Gaebler, *Reinventing Government: How the Entrepreneurial Spirit Is Transforming Government* (New York: Plume, 1993).

14 "Open-source governance" is a political philosophy that advocates the application of the philosophies of the open-source and open-content movements to democratic principles to enable any interested citizen to add to the creation of policy, as with a wiki document. For more on open-source governance see, for example, the Wikipedia summary article on the subject at: https://en.wikipedia.org/wiki/Open-source_governance.

15 Nathaniel Tkacz, "Open Sesame," in *Aeon*, 2013: http://aeon.co/magazine/society/nathaniel-tkacz-open-source-government/.

16 Harlan Cleveland, "The Twilight of Hierarchy: Speculations on the Global Information Society," *Public Administration Review*, 45 (1) (Jan.–Feb. 1984): 185–95.

17 For these and other examples see Australian Public Services Commission *Tackling Wicked Problems* (Canberra: Author, 2007); and John C. Camillus, "Strategy as a Wicked Problem," *Harvard Business Review*, May 2008.

18 Task forces are often used in the private sector to deal with rapid change, or issues that cut across organizational or other boundaries, or (generally) where business-as-usual decision making is not enough. In government, commissions and task forces have been used to inquire into major issues prior to government action. In Canada especially, royal commissions have been used since Confederation to prepare the ground for policy change. Recent examples include the Hall Commission and later the Romanow Commission, which laid the groundwork for the establishment and reform of medicare; the Bilingualism and Biculturalism (B&B) Commission, which led to Canada's official languages policy; the Macdonald Commission, which was an important step toward NAFTA; and many more.

19 To facilitate this dialogue we have created a website at www .CatalyticGovernance.com.

Appendix

1 This appendix is an excerpt from *Scenarios for the Future of the Canadian Payments System*. Reproduced with the permission of the Department of Finance, 2015: http://paymentsystemreview.ca/wp-content/themes/psr-esp-hub/documents/rf_eng.pdf.

Selected Bibliography

Ashby, W.R. *Introduction to Cybernetics*. London: Chapman and Hall, 1956.

Australian Public Services Commission. *Tackling Wicked Problems*. Canberra: Author, 2007.

Bateson, Gregory. *Steps to an Ecology of Mind*. Chicago: University of Chicago Press, 2000.

Bushe, G.R., and A.B. Shani. *Parallel Learning Structures: Increasing Innovation in Bureaucracies*. Boston: Addison-Wesley, 1990.

Camillus, John C. "Strategy as a Wicked Problem." *Harvard Business Review* (May 2008).

Christiansen, Clayton. *The Innovators Dilemma: The Revolutionary Book That Will Change the Way You Do Business*. Boston: Harvard Business School Press, 2000.

Cleveland, Harlan. "The Twilight of Hierarchy: Speculations on the Global Information Society." *Public Administration Review*, 45 (1) (Jan.–Feb. 1984): 185–95.

Davis, Gerald. *Exploring Societal Problems*. Johannesburg: The World Conservation Union Futures Dialogue, IUCN Environment Centre, Johannesburg, SA, 2002.

Davis, Gerald. *Scenarios: An Explorer's Guide*. London: Shell International Limited, 2003.

Davis, Gerald. *Scenarios as a Tool for the 21st Century*. Probing the Future Conference, Strathclyde University, 2002.

Donahue, John D., and Richard J. Zeckhauser. *Collaborative Governance: Private Roles for Public Goals in Turbulent Times*. Princeton, NJ: Princeton University Press, 2011.

Drath, W.H., and C.J. Palus. *Making Common Sense: Leadership as Meaning-Making in a Community of Practice*. Greensboro, NC: Centre for Creative Leadership, 1994.

Edenhofer, O., and M. Kowarsch. "A Pragmatist Concept of Scientific Policy Advice." Working Paper. Berlin: Mercator Research Institute on Global Commons and Climate Change (MCC), (Torgauer Strasse 12–15, 10829), 2012.

Greenwood, D.J., and M. Levin. *Introduction to Action Research*. Thousand Oaks, CA: Sage Publications, 2007.

Habermas, Jürgen. *Toward a Rational Society*. Boston: Beacon Press, 1971.

Hagel, John, III, and John Seely Brown. *The Power of Pull: How Small Moves, Smartly Made, Can Set Big Things in Motion*. New York: Basic Books, 2012.

Haslam, S. Alexander, Stephen D. Reicher, and Michael J. Platow. *The New Psychology of Leadership: Identity, Influence and Power*. New York: Psychology Press, 2011.

Helpman, Elhanan, ed. *General Purpose Technologies and Economic Growth*. Cambridge, MA: MIT Press, 1998.

Lewin, Kurt. "Action Research and Minority Problems." *Journal of Social Issues*, 2 (4) (1946): 34–46.

Luke, Jeffrey S. *Catalytic Leadership: Strategies for an Interconnected World*. San Francisco: Jossey-Bass, 1998.

Martin, Roger L. *The Responsibility Virus: How Control Freaks, Shrinking Violets and the Rest of Us Can Harness the Power of True Partnership*. New York: Basic Books, 2000.

McKinsey Global Institute. *Global Flows in a Digital Age: How Trade, Finance, People and Data Connect the World Economy*. April 2014. Available at: http://www.mckinsey.com/MGI_Globalflows_Full_report_April2014.

Michael, D.N. "Governing by Learning in an Information Society." In Rosell, *Governing in an Information Society*, 121–33.

Mintzberg, Henry, and J.A. Waters. "Of Strategies, Deliberate and Emergent." *Strategic Management Journal*, 6 (3) (Jul.-Sept. 1985): 257–72.

Osborne, David, and Ted Gaebler. *Reinventing Government: How the Entrepreneurial Spirit Is Transforming Government*. New York: Plume, 1993.

Pedler, Mike, ed. *Action Learning in Practice*. Burlington, VT: Gower Publishing, 2012.

Porter, Michael E. "What Is Strategy?" *Harvard Business Review*, 74 (6) (Nov.–Dec. 1996): 61–78.

Rittel, H., and M. Webber. "Dilemmas in a General Theory of Planning." *Policy Sciences*, 4 (1973): 155–69.

Rosell, Steven A., ed. *Governing in an Information Society*. Montreal: Institute for Research on Public Policy, 1992.

Rosell, Steven A. "A Missing Step in the Governance Process." *Development*, 47 (4) (2004): 43.

Rosell, Steven A. *Renewing Governance: Governing by Learning in the Information Age*. Oxford and New York: Oxford University Press, 1999.

Schon, Donald. *Beyond the Stable State*. New York: W.W. Norton, 1973.

Seely Brown, John, and Paul Duguid. *The Social Life of Information*. Cambridge, MA: Harvard Business Review Press, 2002.

Snowden, D.J., and M.D. Boone. "A Leader's Framework for Decision Making." *Harvard Business Review* (November 2007): 69–76.

Task Force for the Payments System Review. *Going Digital: Transitioning to Digital Payments*. 2011. See: http://paymentsystemreview.ca/wp-content/themes/psr-esp-hub/documents/r03_eng.pdf.

Task Force for the Payments System Review. *Moving Canada into the Digital Age*. 2011. See: http://paymentsystemreview.ca/wp-content/themes/psr-esp-hub/documents/rf_eng.pdf.

Trist, Eric, et al., eds. *The Social Engagement of Social Science*. 3 vols. Philadelphia, PA: University of Pennsylvania Press, 1990–7.

Viewpoint Learning, in association with the Scenarios Roundtable and the Canadian Task Force for the Payments System Review. *Scenarios for the Future of the Canadian Payments System*. 2011. See: http://paymentsystem-review.ca/wp-content/themes/psr-esp-hub/documents/r01_eng.pdf.

Wenger, Etienne. *Communities of Practice: Learning, Meaning, and Identity*. Cambridge: Cambridge University Press, 1998.

Westley, Frances, Michael Q. Patton, and Brenda Zimmerman. *Getting to Maybe: How the World Is Changed*. Toronto: Vintage Canada, 2007.

Whyte, William F., ed. *Participatory Action Research*. Thousand Oaks, CA: Sage, 1991.

Winnicott, D.W. *Playing and Reality*. London: Tavistock, 1971.

Yankelovich, Daniel. *The Magic of Dialogue*. New York: Simon and Schuster, 2001.

Yankelovich, Daniel. *Wicked Problems, Workable Solutions: Lessons from a Public Life*. Lanham, MD: Rowman and Littlefield, 2014.

About the Authors

It has been quite a journey. What began as an effort to devise and implement significant changes to Canada's payments system became a case study of developing better approaches to leading and governing in the information age. The authors came to this effort from different starting points, backgrounds, and interests.

Starting Points

Starting Point: Pat Meredith

Payments are a passion of mine. In February 2010, when Finance Minister Flaherty asked me to chair the Task Force for the Payments System Review, I accepted without hesitation. As a former senior bank executive and adviser, I understood the importance of payments to the Canadian economy and to the banks that were the dominant players in the Canadian payments system. But the fact that I pursued it as vigorously as I did stemmed from the realization that, for Canadians to participate fully in the digital economy, Canada needed to build a digital payments foundation for the future.

Massive changes were already under way in payments systems in other areas of the world. Given the speed of that change and the resulting uncertainties, the Payments Task Force realized early that fulfilling its mandate would require more than the usual analytic approach, and that we would need to engage the experience, expertise, and perspectives of industry experts and key stakeholders. More importantly, we realized that the process had to be open and inclusive; it had to use dialogue to break down the barriers result-ing from different assumptions and beliefs about the future; and it had to produce at least one desired outcome that the community could embrace. Finally, the output had to belong to the payments industry, not just to a task force.

Given these realizations, I turned to Steven Rosell, who had facilitated dialogue/scenarios processes on the Future of Canada and on Renewing Governance that had made a huge impression on me. They had changed my thinking dramatically.

Starting Point: Steven Rosell

For over thirty years, I have pursued the question of how groups, or-ganizations, and societies learn, and how that affects the way we orga-nize and govern ourselves. That question has been central to my work as a senior government official, researcher, author, and co-founder of a company in Canada and the United States that focuses on applica-tions of dialogue.[1]

Beginning in the late 1980s, I organized a series of roundtable projects that created spaces where leaders from different sectors could engage in dialogue and undertake experiments, especially about the challenges of governing amidst the complex of social and technological changes that define "the information society." The results of this work were published in three books and numer-ous articles.

I met Pat Meredith when she was an especially strong and in-sightful member of two of those roundtables. As the executive vice-president of a major Canadian bank, she had a reputation as the leading strategist in the banking sector. Pat approached me in early 2010 to talk about the potential of using a roundtable process, including both dialogue and scenarios, in the work of Canada's Task Force for the Payments System Review, which she had just

---

1 That company, Viewpoint Learning, was co-founded with Daniel Yan-kelovich, a dean of public opinion research and an authority on using dialogue and on how societies learn. Viewpoint Learning develops special-ized applications of dialogue to enable groups of leaders to work together more effectively and to better engage the public.

agreed to chair. As we talked, it seemed to me that this would be a tremendous opportunity not only to significantly advance the work of the Payments Task Force, but also to test and further develop the dialogue/scenario process and the art of governing in an information society.

When using scenarios, I have always partnered with an experienced scenario practitioner, and for this project I suggested we bring in the best: Ged Davis, who had been vice-president at Shell International and led Shell's path-breaking scenario team, and then created the scenario practice of the World Economic Forum in Davos. Ged and I had worked together on some smaller projects. This would be an opportunity to work together on something bigger.

Starting Point: Ged Davis

Much of my early work on scenarios at Shell was focused on assisting executive teams and boards to better understand both the risks faced by their businesses and the potential for change. At the heart of the work was devising ways of improving the quality of corporate governance.

In the 1990s I began to experiment with developing scenario-building processes with large groups (50 to 80 participants) representing a wide range of organizations, and focused on different countries and subject areas, including energy, sustainable development, environment, the digital revolution, and health.[2] The basis of the approach for all these projects was a four-step process: framing, scenarios building, scenarios confirmation, and scenarios use.

My interest in the detailed design of scenario development processes led me to the work of Steven Rosell and his colleague Daniel Yankelovich at Viewpoint Learning. They had pioneered dialogue applications to many situations, and dialogue is the central

---

2 A good example was the scenarios developed with the World Business Council for Sustainable Development – consisting of some 200 international companies – which led to a new vision for the WBCSD as a catalyst for change. See Lloyd Timberlake/World Business Council for Sustainable Development, *Catalyzing Change: A Short History of the WBCSD* (Conches-Geneva: World Business Council for Sustainable Development, 2006), 24–7.

communication mode for scenario development. We worked together on a number of small projects and wanted to work together on a larger project with significant dialogue and scenarios-building components. When Steve indicated in early 2010 that he was involved in discussions about a project on the future of financial payments we agreed that this might be the right project to work on together. For me this brought together two intriguing possibilities: using the four-step process with an enhanced dialogue approach, and addressing the development of digital payments systems – an aspect of the digital revolution that particularly interested me.

The "Payments Scenarios Roundtable" got under way in August 2010. My hope was that this would be a leading-edge example of the application of dialogue-based methods to scenarios building and use and that the project would make a material contribution to the work of the Canadian Payments Task Force. That this collaboration would lead to a reframing of scenario processes as part of a broader picture – *catalytic governance* – was both unexpected and exciting.

Leading Change

From these different starting points, and drawing on decades of experience in dialogue, scenario planning, strategy/policy development, and governance, we came together to create and facilitate a process to resolve the governance challenges and "wicked problems" of the Canadian payments system. This was very much a collaborative effort to which we each contributed,[3] working together to lead and catalyse transformative change.

We believe that the catalytic governance approach that emerged from this effort, and which is described in this volume, provides a powerful way to make progress on the many "wicked problems" we now face around the world. We see the publication of this book as a contribution to a growing global dialogue about transforming leadership and governance in the information age.

---

3 The authors of this volume are listed in the chronological order in which we joined this effort.

Index

Page references followed by *fig* indicate figures; page references followed by *t* indicate tables.